SLATES FRO
ABERGYNOLWYN

The Story of Bryneglwys Slate Quarry

by

ALAN HOLMES

GWYNEDD ARCHIVES SERVICE

First Impression: August 1986
Second Impression: October 1986

ISBN 0 901 337 42 0

Cover designed by Magma Designs, Beaumaris

Published by Gwynedd Archives Service, County Offices, Caernarfon, Gwynedd.
Printed by Gee and Son, Ltd., Denbigh, Clwyd

I've got great respect for the generation that has gone.

— Mr. Caradog Jones, 1904-1982,
Bryneglwys quarryman.

Contents

ABBREVIATIONS

CRO — Caernarfon Record Office
DRO — Dolgellau Record Office
NLW — National Library of Wales
PRO — Public Record Office
UCNW — University College of North Wales, Bangor

LIST OF PLATES

LIST OF FIGURES

ACKNOWLEDGEMENTS

I WOULD like to record my thanks to the following people for help in preparing this book:

For providing copious lists of documentary sources, extracts from Parliamentary Papers (annual statistics) and much else, including reading the draft manuscript, my sincere thanks go to J. S. Wilkinson. In the field, considerable effort was contributed by R. Thomas, both in the survey and especially the photographic work, above and below ground. M. R. Harrison also contributed to the field work. My late wife Joan conducted interviews, assisted with survey work and provided support and encouragement throughout.

The staffs of the National Library of Wales, Aberystwyth; Gwynedd Archives Service, Dolgellau and Caernarfon Record Offices; University College of North Wales, Bangor; Central Reference Library, Bristol; Public Record Office; British Library Newpaper Library, Colindale, were very helpful in dealing with my queries.

Local residents who have given freely of their reminiscences and other data — Caradog Jones, Herbert Jones, Lewis Roberts, Glyn Felix Williams, Mrs. R. O. Williams (all now deceased); Griffith Evans, Rhys Gruffydd, Mrs. M. Hamer, Hugh Jones, Peter Roberts, Mr. C. Jones and Mrs. R. Roberts.

Assistance with Welsh translations — Richard Evans, Rhys Gruffydd, Gareth Lewis.

Photographs — J. H. L. Adams, G. Braithwaite, M. R. Harrison, Caradog Jones, D. J. Mitchell, J. B. Snell.

Loan of surveying instruments — J. L. H. Bate.

Miscellaneous information — E. D. Chambers, T. England, S. Jackson, O. H. Prosser, J. N. Slater and other members of the TRPS too numerous to mention individually, who have helped in many ways. Alison Lewis kindly provided data from her own research at Bryneglwys.

Preface

MANY thousands of men spent their working lives in the North Wales slate industry, over a period spanning several generations, yet very few quarries remain active today. Modern factory-made substitutes have largely replaced slate for roofing and with the decline of quarrying a distinctive way of life has disappeared. Abergynolwyn Quarry, also known as Bryneglwys, lay in the Southern Merionethshire slate district and this book records the story from its beginnings in the 1840s to final closure over a century later. Today forest plantations have engulfed the site, yet it once provided work for 300 men and was the mainstay of Abergynolwyn village.

The Talyllyn Railway was built to serve the quarry, and when it came near to closure in 1950 a preservation society was formed, the first of its kind to take on the task of controlling and running a public passenger-carrying railway. As there were many slate quarries working at that time, the demise of Bryneglwys aroused little interest, especially as resources were fully stretched in keeping the wheels turning on the railway. Later, in the early 1970s, a greater awareness of a disappearing industry was stimulated by, for example, the opening to the public of the Dinorwic Quarry Workshop and the Llechwedd Quarry Museum.

In Abergynolwyn the late Mr. Caradog Jones, a retired Bryneglwys quarryman, opened a small village museum whose contents included the bell, foundation stone, tools and other small relics saved from the quarry and village. Further interest was aroused by the Talyllyn Railway extension to Nant Gwernol, opened in 1976, which brought passengers to the foot of the incline on the former quarry tramway. Meanwhile, the quarry sheds and workings were deteriorating and so it was decided to gather material for a study of the quarry in depth before too much was lost. The results are presented in this book.

Material for the study has come from three main sources. Firstly, from the site itself which was surveyed using simple but adequate techniques. Buildings and other structures were measured, photographed and sketched; underground workings surveyed with compass and chain; levels established by theodolite; maps made by plane table, compass, clinometer and tape backed up by aerial photographs. The task of surveying was made lighter by the practical help of several people, notably Dick Thomas and Ross Harrison, and benefited by experience gained under the tutorship of Dr. M. J. T. Lewis on an industrial archaeology field course in North Wales.

Our survey of the buildings proved timely. A correspondent of the *Carnarvon and Denbigh Herald,* visiting the quarry in 1873 remarked in passing that he also viewed the nearby 'ancient ruins' of Castell-y-Bere, destroyed by Edward I in the thirteenth century. Today's visitor will see far more of Llewellyn's castle, still standing, than he will of the mills, cabans and barracks of Bryneglwys and Braichgoch. Quarry buildings once vacated have been plundered for their roof slates, timber and fittings and finally bulldozed lest visitors injure themselves clambering over the ruins.

The second source of information is documentary material. Unfortunately the Company records — minute books, correspondence files, etc. — have not survived, but a thorough search of papers in various repositories has yielded enough data to establish the main events of the Company's history, for example the terms of the quarry leases. Wherever possible, original source material has been used and in doing so information published in previous works has been found to be inaccurate in some cases. In this connection I would like to record my grateful thanks to Jeremy Wilkinson, who has made freely available the fruits of his extensive searches in Record Offices and Libraries up and down the land in pursuit of data relating to mines and quarries in North Wales.

The other main source of data comes from our many conversations with former quarrymen, their families and friends. Some, alas, are no longer with us and our tape recordings and notes form an irreplaceable link with them. Mr. Caradog Jones is particularly remembered for the fund of memories which he gave us. Some of this material was gathered by Alison Lewis, who has generously made available the results of her own research at Bryneglwys. Large-scale copies of the drawings in this book have been deposited with the Gwynedd Archives Service at Dolgellau Record Office, together with other data acquired in the course of the research.

During the active life of the quarry the spellings of some Welsh place-names were different to those in use today. When quoting directly from contemporary sources, the spellings are as given in the original documents, in the interests of accuracy. Otherwise, place names are rendered according to the *Gazetteer of Welsh Place Names* published by the University of Wales Press.

In the course of our research, much help has been received from members of the Talyllyn Railway Preservation Society and others, which is gratefully acknowledged. A list of contributors is given on page 8. My late wife, Joan, provided practical help and support at all stages, and I dedicate this book to her memory.

1

General History

WELSH roofing slate has been used in Britain for hundreds of years, but it really came into its own in the nineteenth century, when the great industrial towns grew up around the mills and factories which mushroomed in the wake of the Industrial Revolution. The demand for workers' housing led to a need for cheap materials and the slate industry responded by expanding output on a large scale, annual production reaching nearly half a million tonnes by the end of the century.

In 1800 there was already an established trade in slates from the Caernarvonshire quarries, and in the next fifty years the slate veins were tapped at many more places including Bryneglwys in Southern Merionethshire. (The former counties of Caernarvon and Merioneth now form part of Gwynedd). New technology was needed to enable the industry to cope with the increased demand, and the adoption of rail transport in which the Welsh quarries were innovators, was arguably the most important single advance. Slate quarries were often located in remote, inaccessible uplands and tramways provided a cheap and efficient means of getting the slates from quarry to quayside, main line railway or road.

Bryneglwys Slate Quarry began as one of the many small workings on the fringe of the Corris District. The main quarries of the area, notably Braichgoch, Gaewern and Aberllefenni were clustered around Corris in the Dulas Valley and Bryneglwys only grew to become one of the largest Mid-Wales quarries after a substantial capital investment by the Aberdovey Slate Company Limited and the construction of the Talyllyn Railway in the 1860s. At its peak Bryneglwys accounted for 30 per cent of the Corris District output.

The area, which is shown on the map in figure 1, lies between the rivers Mawddach and Dyfi, extending from the coast of Cardigan Bay eastwards for 20 miles (32 km) to Dinas Mawddwy. The ridge of Cader Idris dominates the northern part of this upland region, whilst in the south a range of rock-crested grassy hills rises to nearly 2,200 ft. (670 m) at the summit of Tarren-y-Gesail.

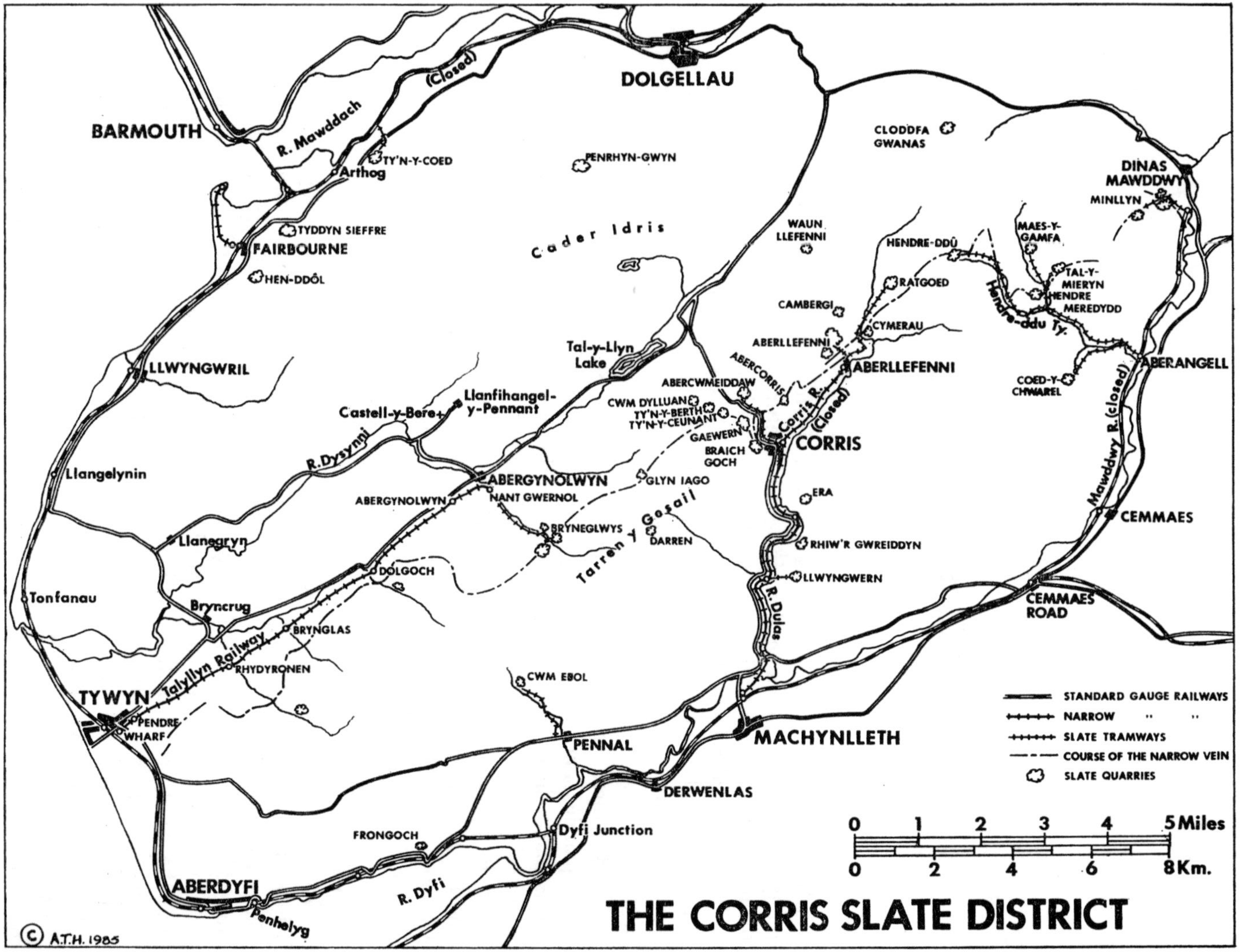
THE CORRIS SLATE DISTRICT
BARMOUTH
DOLGELLAU
R. Mawddach
(Closed)
TY'N-Y-COED
Arthog
PENRHYN-GWYN
TYDDYN SIEFFRE
FAIRBOURNE
HEN-DDÔL
Cader Idris
CLODDFA GWANAS
DINAS MAWDDWY
MINLLYN
WAUN LLEFENNI
HENDRE-DDÛ
MAES-Y-GAMFA
TAL-Y-MIERYN
HENDRE MEREDYDD
Hendre-ddu Ty.
RATGOED
CAMBERGI
CYMERAU
ABERLLEFENNI
ABERCORRIS
ABERCWMEIDDAW
CWM DYLLUAN
TY'N-Y-BERTH
TY'N-Y-CEUNANT
GAEWERN
BRAICH GOCH
Corris R.
(Closed)
CORRIS
COED-Y-CHWAREL
Mawddwy R. (closed)
ABERANGELL
CEMMAES
Tal-y-Llyn Lake
LLWYNGWRIL
Castell-y-Bere
Llanfihangel-y-Pennant
R. Dysynni
Llangelynin
ABERGYNOLWYN
NANT GWERNOL
GLYN IAGO
ERA
Tarren y Gesail
BRYNEGLWYS
DARREN
RHIW'R GWREIDDYN
LLWYNGWERN
Llanegryn
DOLGOCH
Tonfanau
Bryncrug
R. Dulas
CEMMAES ROAD
BRYNGLAS
Talyllyn Railway
RHYDYRONEN
CWM EBOL
TYWYN
PENDRE
WHARF
PENNAL
MACHYNLLETH
DERWENLAS
FRONGOCH
Dyfi Junction
ABERDYFI
R. Dyfi
Penhelyg
STANDARD GAUGE RAILWAYS
NARROW " "
SLATE TRAMWAYS
COURSE OF THE NARROW VEIN
SLATE QUARRIES
0 1 2 3 4 5 Miles
0 2 4 6 8 Km.
© A.T.H. 1985

Figure 1

The A487 is the only metalled road to cross the area from north to south, and between Corris and Machynlleth it follows the winding course of the River Dulas, a tributary of the Dyfi. Corris lies 5½ miles (9 km) north of Machynlleth, and Aberllefenni is situated a short distance further upstream along the Dulas. It was at Aberllefenni that one of the earliest and most important slate quarries was established, reputedly in Tudor times and it remains as the only working quarry in the district at the time of writing.

Several quarries near Corris were active in a small way in the first half of the nineteenth century, but their development was limited by the poor transport available. Slate is a heavy material in relation to its market value, so the cost of transport was a dominant factor in determining the success or failure of a quarry, no matter how good the slate. Slates were carted along rough roads from the quarries to the river port of Derwenlas on the highest navigable reach of the Dyfi, 2½ miles (4 km) below Machynlleth. From the more inaccessible quarries they began their laborious journey on pack animals or sledges which were brought down steep mountain paths to the nearest road. From Derwenlas small river craft took the slates to the port of Aberdyfi where they were transhipped yet again into sea-going trading vessels for distribution to coastal and inland ports around the British Isles.[1] The Aberdovey Custom House Book records that slate was exported to Chester in the 1790s, 36,000 slates being sent in 1793.[2]

By 1833 shipments of slate from Derwenlas had reached 1,500 tons per annum, and in the 1850s several proposals were made for a railway connection between the quarries and the Dyfi wharves, to cut the cost of transport.[3] One such scheme was the Aberdovey Railway of 1850 which would have terminated at a wharf to be built at Pant Eidal on the north shore, where sea-going vessels could load directly.[4] In the event however it was the Corris, Machynlleth and River Dovey Tramroad (later the Corris Railway, closed in 1948) which was actually built, opening in 1859 and connecting with the quays at Derwenlas. This gave the quarries at Corris, Aberllefenni and Ratgoed a decisive advantage over others, such as Bryneglwys, which depended on more primitive methods to get their products to market.

The long straight valley between Cader Idris and Tarren-y-Gesail bears no name upon the Ordnance Survey map, but geologists call it, aptly, the Talyllyn Valley. It lies along the line of the Bala fault and was formed, or at least deepened, by glacial erosion. The River Dysynni flows down the Talyllyn Valley as far as Abergynolwyn, where it turns abruptly northwards to pass through a narrow gorge into the Dyffryn Dysynni and then flows placidly seawards to Broad Water. Another legacy of glaciation is the series of 'hanging valleys' along the south side of the Talyllyn Valley, whose energetic streams have cut deep ravines such as Nant Dolgoch with its popular waterfalls and

[1] NLW Machynlleth Deeds Box 25, Bill of Complaint in Chancery, 23 July 1855.
[2] *NLW Journal*, Summer 1973 (Transcribed from NLW 20702 C).
[3] DRO Qr/r/(xx), Map of Corris, Machynlleth, Aberdovey and Towyn Railway, 1852.
[4] DRO.

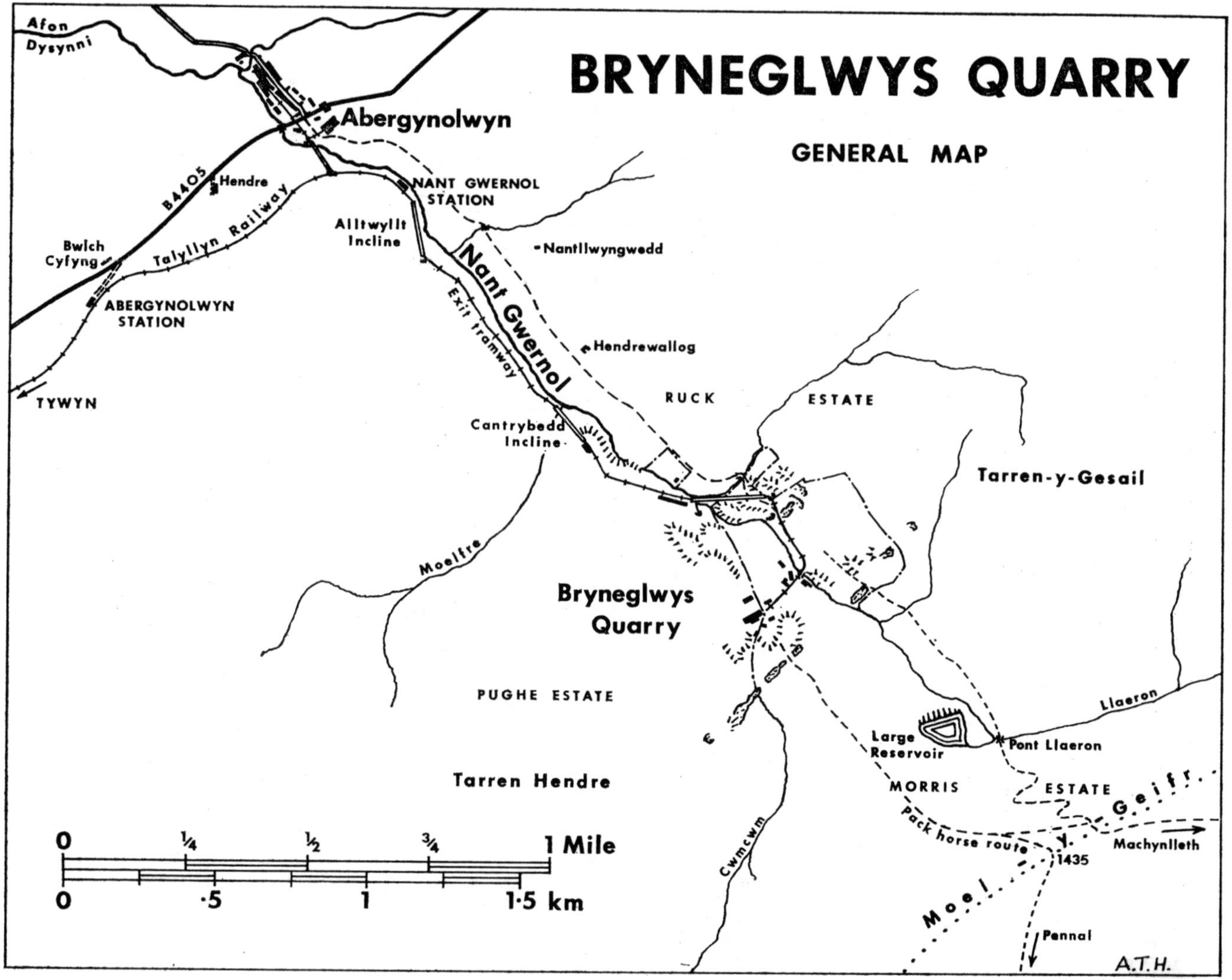
BRYNEGLWYS QUARRY
GENERAL MAP
Afon Dysynni
Abergynolwyn
B4405
Hendre
Bwlch Cyfyng
Talyllyn Railway
ABERGYNOLWYN STATION
TYWYN
NANT GWERNOL STATION
Alltwyllt Incline
Nant Gwernol
Exit tramway
Nantllwyngwedd
Hendrewallog
RUCK
ESTATE
Cantrybedd Incline
Moelfre
Bryneglwys Quarry
PUGHE ESTATE
Tarren Hendre
Tarren-y-Gesail
Large Reservoir
Pont Llaeron
Llaeron
MORRIS
ESTATE
Pack horse route
Geifr
Moel y
1435
Machynlleth
Pennal
Cwmcwm
0
1/4
1/2
3/4
1 Mile
0
·5
1
1·5 km
A.T.H.

Figure 2

Nant Gwernol opposite Abergynolwyn village. It was across the upper reaches of the Gwernol, shown on the map in figure 2, that Bryneglwys Quarry lay.

The headwaters of the Gwernol are the Llaeron and Cwmcwm or 'Boundary Stream' which drain off the slopes of Moel-y-Geifr. This 1,400 foot (427 m) ridge forms the barrier which stood in the way of direct rail access from Bryneglwys to the Dyfi wharves. Bryn-yr-Eglwys, later contracted to Bryneglwys, means literally a church on rising ground but no such building is known to have existed there. The name may have been associated with an ancient stone circle, originally situated where the New Mill was subsequently built, and which the quarry manager removed to a spot 40 yards away in the 1860s. Some fir trees were planted within the circle on its new site, and today these trees including a huge monkey-puzzle tower above the more juvenile plantings in the Forestry Commission's Dyfi Forest.[5]

Bryneglwys Farm existed in 1834 and lay on one of the three estates concerned in the quarry's history, the others being Cantrybedd and Hendre-wallog. All were in the parish of Llanfihangel-y-Pennant, but the divided ownership of the quarry land was to become a source of frustration and expense to the quarry proprietors. They had to obtain separate leases for each estate, relations with the landlords were sometimes strained and much money was spent on lawyer's fees. As the late Mr. Caradog Jones, a retired Bryneglwys quarryman put it:

> There was a bit of bother now and again especially when the owners of the different estates were visiting the quarry. They wanted to know how many chambers were working on their estates. A rumour came round and we stopped working in certain chambers for the day to save paying royalty. That was playing havoc in the quarry; for every three trucks of slates sent down the track there, they claimed one for royalty so no wonder the wages were a bit low.

The Bryneglwys Estate was owned by Lewis Morris of Machynlleth and formed a roughly triangular piece of land covering 439 acres (178 hectares) bounded by the ridge of Moel-y-Geifr, the Llaeron and the Boundary Stream. Part of it extended beyond the Llaeron, between Nant-y-Nod and an un-named brook 750 yards (686 m) upstream. The Boundary Stream is now a mis-nomer since its diversion by the quarry proprietors, but originally it formed the boundary between Bryneglwys and Cantrybedd.

Cantrybedd or Cae-yn-trybedd (derivation unknown) was owned by the Rev. Richard Pughe of Llanfihangel-y-Gwynt, Montgomeryshire. The estate extended along the southern slopes of the Gwernol ravine to a boundary beyond the Tywyn-Abergynolwyn road, one of the buildings at Hendre bearing a tablet reading 'Rev. Richard Pughe built AD 1840'. The third property was Hendre-wallog, owned by the Ruck family of Pant Lludw, Pennal, and lay east of the Llaeron having common borders with each of the other estates. The title Abergynolwyn Quarries was frequently used to describe the complete works; some-

[5] *Royal Commission on the Ancient Monuments of Wales and Monmouthshire*, p. 114. Also in NLW 18602 D.

times they were referred to as 'Bryneglwys and Cantrybedd Quarries', and often simply Bryneglwys Quarry.

So far as has been discovered, the earliest lease was granted by Lewis Morris to John Pughe of Bronhaulwen, Penegoes in 1844 though there is a tradition that Pughe had purchased an interest in the quarry, possibly a takenote (a right to prospect for a limited time) from a few workmen for £120.[6] The terms of the 1844 lease provided for a fixed annual rent of £40 for a period of fifty years from the 12 November 1844. Under the terms of the lease, Pughe agreed to make compensation for any damage to grass, herbage, etc., resulting from quarry operations such as tipping, the damages to be assessed at half-yearly intervals by indifferent persons nominated by each party.[7] The terms were moderate and did not provide for the usual royalty based upon the annual tonnage of slate produced, which suggests that Morris thought the land of little value as a mineral property.

Pughe got a tougher bargain in the case of Cantrybedd, which he leased for sixty years from 31 December 1846, although we don't know the precise terms. When the Aberdovey Slate Company bought the lease in 1864 they negotiated fresh terms as the existing ones were 'too onerous'.[8]

John Pughe came from Carmarthen, and he partnered his wife's brother, Hugh Williams of Machynlleth, in a lead mining venture at Dylife, Montgomeryshire, which prospered in the 1840s. At Bryneglwys he set about the tasks of 'driving levels, making roads, bridges and other conveniences' and erecting a mill. He placed an advertisement in the *Mining Journal* inviting subscriptions for 2,400 shares, the remaining 2,600 to be retained by the proprietor:

> As the shares will be sold so low, as to admit almost the humblest individual to make purchases, the proprietor begs to add, that he will not be disposed to admit any partners except such as are very respectable, and to sell no person less than 20 shares . . . [9]

Little is known about Pughe, except that he died very soon afterwards, his widow Anne carrying on as proprietress for some years. At the time of her husband's death they lived in Aberdyfi where she remained, with her sister and daughter, and was to make a handsome profit from the undertaking when she sold out to the Aberdovey Slate Company.

The quarry was evidently successful for a few years, as in 1851 twenty-four men were employed. The census returns for that year show that there were six quarrymen from Llanllyfni, Caernarvonshire, lodging in the district and the Agent was George Smith of Amport, Hampshire. We conjecture that the Llanllyfni men were slatemakers and rockmen brought in because of a shortage of local craftsmen, but it is an interesting coincidence that another Llanllyfni man, J. Ll. Jones, acquired an interest in the quarry in 1862.

[6] R. P. Morris, *Cantref Meirionydd*, Dolgellau, 1890, p. 540.
[7] DRO Z/M/2359/7, Indenture between Lewis Morris and John Pughe.
[8] PRO C31/1961 Part 2, Affidavits in Re Williams and Parry (Trustees), No. 2254.
[9] *Mining Journal* Vol. xvii, No. 631, 25 September 1847, p 449.

The history of the quarry becomes difficult to trace in the 1850s, but it is believed to have been worked for a time by a Mr. Davies of Corris under some arrangement with Mrs. Pughe. A report on the quarry was written in glowing terms by George Smith in 1857, obviously intended for prospective purchasers.[10] In 1859 Edward Davies of Dolcaradog, a noted operator in the metal mining industry of Mid-Wales, was approached on behalf of Mrs. Pughe to find a buyer for the quarry. The purchase price asked was £11,000, Davies to take a 2½ per cent fee plus 7 per cent for any sum over that figure.[11] Whether he accepted the commission or not is not known, but by summer 1862 it had come to the notice of John Lloyd Jones of Baladaulyn, Llanllyfni. He was the son of the Rev. John Jones of Talysarn, a well-known quarryman turned preacher. Jones senior was a shareholder and also in 1851 the manager of Dorothea Quarry, then owned by a syndicate of quarrymen. J. Ll. Jones had various quarrying interests, operating under the title 'Britannia Slate and Slab Company', and in 1863 he was manager of the Pen-yr-Orsedd Quarry, selling out to W. A. Darbyshire & Co. in that year. His attention later turned to other quarries in the Corris District, notably Llwyngwern and Glandulas whose leases he acquired in 1867.[12] He was something of a wheeler-dealer, acquiring quarries having good prospects but lacking capital for development, and after making some improvements selling out to a company.

J. Ll. Jones first visited Bryneglwys with Robert Williams, a Llanllyfni quarryman who has left an account of the proceedings in his autobiography.[13] They travelled by coach to Talyllyn and looked through the quarry the following day accompanied by Robert Hughes, the manager of Aberllefenni Quarry. They were impressed wih what they saw and Jones decided to negotiate for a lease. The quarry was not being worked at the time, and shortly afterwards a summary agreement was drawn up with Mrs. Pughe's solicitors Messrs Howell and Morgan and sealed, under which Jones took an underlease at a royalty of one-twelfth in respect of Bryneglwys. There was prolonged haggling over the valuation of the quarry machinery, stocks, etc., and Mrs. Pughe tried unsuccessfully to stop her lawyers from effecting the conveyance. Williams tells how he and Robert Hughes, who had been engaged as the Pughe's valuer, compared notes privately and allowed Hughes's valuation to be somewhat higher than Jones's. They were taken unexpectedly one day to meet Mrs. Pughe and her sister in the presence of their lawyers and Hughes was asked to state his figure. He replied that he could not remember and would have brought the account with him if he had known of the meeting beforehand. In reply to the same question Williams quoted J. Ll. Jones's offer. This was regarded as too small by half, but he pointed out that the machinery etc., was old by then. Hughes said he thought his valuation was higher.

[10] *NLW Annual Report,* 1973-4, p. 38, Deposit of Edward Davies Papers, Report by George Smith.

[11] *NLW Annual Report,* 1973-4, p. 38, Deposit of Edward Davies Papers, Letters re sale of Bryneglwys Quarry.

[12] UCNW, Nantlle Mss.

[13] NLW Ms. 8412, Autobiography of Robert Williams, Towyn.

> 'I hope that is the case Mr. Hughes' said Mrs. Pughe's sister. 'Yes indeed' said Mr. Howell, with a smile. Then, taking their arms Howell stepped between Hughes and Williams and prevented them from speaking with each other. But Mr. Morgan's dog was an old dog and his purpose was too late . . .

In the end they agreed to split the difference between the two figures, but David Howell had the last laugh — he was to inherit Mrs. Pughe's fortune later.

The quarry was worked under this agreement from October 1862 with six men, rising to twenty-three in December. Their wages ranged from 2/2d. to 3/4d. per day (11p to 16½p), most receiving 2/6d. (12½p). By 1863 J. Ll. Jones had 'organised gentlemen of sufficient means to enable the quarry to be opened on a grand and effective scale' as Williams put it, meaning the Aberdovey Slate Company Limited, registered on 23 January 1864. Its origins were in the Manchester cotton industry.

One of the largest cotton spinning firms in the country at that time was McConnel and Kennedy whose mill was at Ancoats, Manchester. In 1860 the partners were the McConnel brothers William, Henry and James but by the following year William had become the sole proprietor. By 1863 it seems that he had decided to diversify his interests, possibly it has been suggested because of the threat to the supply of raw cotton posed by the American Civil War. He chose to cash in on the demand for roofing slates which accompanied the rapid expansion of the industrial towns of the time. We don't know how he was introduced to Bryneglwys, presumably as a result of J. Ll. Jones's efforts, but together with his brothers and associates he formed the Aberdovey Slate Company Limited with a capital of £75,000 in 750 shares of £100 each. It was a limited liability company constituted under the Companies Act of 1862.[14]

All but two of the original shareholders lived in or near Manchester and the Managing Director and largest shareholder was Thomas Houldsworth McConnel, brother of William. The new owners realised that one of the first necessities for success was rail access, for the *Carnarvon and Denbigh Herald* of 30 January 1864 noted that 'James Swinton Spooner was surveying for a narrow-gauge tramway from Towyn to Bryneglwys Quarry', and by April they reported that construction work was in progress. The advance of the main line railway to Tywyn in November 1863, albeit on an isolated section from Aberdyfi to Llwyngwril, meant that McConnel's tramway only needed to be laid thus far and not to Aberdyfi, although it did of course result in the slates having to be transhipped due to the break of gauge. Meanwhile, Bryneglwys slate had to be carted down by road and McConnel offered to pay £10 to the Trustees of the Tywyn to Talyllyn turnpike for every £50 which they spent on the road.[15]

The Aberdovey Slate Company's contractual right to the quarry seems to have begun formally on 25 March 1864, the effective date of commencement of the leases, though they may have made a provisional agreement with J. Ll. Jones

[14] PRO BT 31/881/932c, Memorandum of Association of the Aberdovey Slate Company Limited.
[15] *Merionethshire Herald,* 23 April 1864.

to allow them to start work earlier. They purchased the Bryneglwys and Cantrybedd quarry leases from Mrs. Pughe and her daughter Maria, the legal representatives of the late John Pughe. The new company agreed to buy them out for £11,850, the purchase being confirmed at a special shareholders meeting on 26 April 1864.[16] They paid a further £27,000 for John Lloyd Jones's interests, including the quarry machinery, mills, tramways, etc. The total cost to the Company was thus nearly £40,000 which seems very large in view of the limited extent to which it had been developed, but reflects the optimism they had in the potential profitability of the slate veins. At that time there was a boom in mining investment in Wales and fortunes were made at the expense of speculators who were only too ready to part with their money on the promises of an eloquent prospectus. Robert Williams claimed that J. Ll. Jones had spent less than £1,000 on the quarry, probably an exaggeration but he undoubtedly made a very large profit, as did the Pughes.

The Company set about expanding the works energetically, driving new levels, opening chambers and increasing the mill capacity. They retained Robert Williams as Agent, working at first according to a plan drawn up by James Wyatt, Lord Penrhyn's Agent. Williams decided however that he knew better, so he approached T. H. McConnel who said that he had not yet approved Wyatt's plan. McConnel told Williams to carry on with his scheme, but only after a meeting at Bryneglwys with Wyatt who, according to Williams's account, accepted the new plan when it was explained to him.

A local newspaper records that in July 1866 Richard Lewis retired and received a clock and silver inkstand worth 29 guineas (£30.45) as a mark of esteem for the 'brief period in which he held the superintendence of the works' at Bryneglwys Quarry.[17] Who he was and what his relationship was with Robert Williams is not clear.

The Cantrybedd lease acquired by the Company contained terms which they considered excessive, so they negotiated with the landlords for a new lease. Following the death of the Rev. Richard Pughe in 1858 the mineral rights and royalties were shared among his seven surviving children, including Charlotte who had married in 1862. Her share had been incorporated in the marriage settlement and Chancery proceedings were necessary before the old lease could be surrendered. Two new leases were drawn up, one for Charlotte's share and the other for her six brothers and sisters, the terms amounting to a total annual rent of £200 minimum or one-fifteenth of the slates produced.

To allow development of the Broad Vein, part of Hendrewallog was leased for forty-five years from 1 May 1866 at the same royalty but a minimum rent of £50. The Ruck land on the Narrow Vein was two-thirds leased and one-third conveyed freehold, the terms of the leasehold being similar to the Broad Vein lease except that it became renewable annually after twenty-four years. On Bryneglwys the Company secured the right to work minerals other than

16 PRO BT 31/881/923c, Special Resolutions of the Aberdovey Slate Company Limited, 8 April and 26 April 1864.

17 *Carnarvon and Denbigh Herald*, 7 July 1866.

slate for twenty-nine years from 12 November 1865 at one-twelfth royalty. This lease was treated as a dead letter, metallic ores not being found in workable quantities. They also leased Bryneglwys Farm at an annual rent of £60 which allowed them to produce hay, etc., and to stable their horses conveniently close to the quarry.[18]

The Company leased two further pieces of land on the Pughe estate, paying an annual rent of £9 for forty-five years from 25 March 1864. One allowed them to deposit spoil outside the entrance to the Long Tunnel, the other formed the bed of the tramway from the stream at the foot of Cantrybedd Incline to the Village Incline east points. They needed to provide housing for the quarrymen and their families, so they purchased the freehold of a large piece of land for £350 from the Rev. G. R. G. Pughe, eldest son of the late Richard Pughe. This included the bed of the tramway from the Talyllyn Railway boundary east of Abergynolwyn Station as far as the Village Incline east points, the incline, Abergynolwyn Village and Nantllwyngwedd Farm. The tramway lease and the conveyance contained covenants securing to the Pughes the right to use the line for the carriage of minerals etc. at minimum rates.[19]

The expenses of development in these early years on top of the original cost of acquisition greatly exceeded the Company's expectations, so they raised further capital by way of a one for one rights issue of £50 shares. Of the sixteen shareholders in the original list nine were merchants, three textile manufacturers, one a civil engineer and two were gentlemen. All except two had addresses in the Manchester area and one-third of the shares were registered in the names of the McConnels. The secretary was T. R. S. Cannon whose office was at 30 Pall Mall, Manchester. By 1867 £99,000 of the issued capital of £112,500 had been paid up and in July of that year the Company name was changed to The Abergynolwyn Slate Company Limited. Still the expenditure continued to rise and in November the Directors were authorised to raise yet more capital, this time in 7½ per cent preference shares, £16,500 worth being issued in October 1869.[20] By 1874 the secretary was James Stevens of 88 Mosley Street, Manchester.

Thomas Houldsworth McConnel spent much of his time at Brynhyfryd, Tywyn, during the development of the quarry and the building of the Talyllyn Railway. In May 1869 he was granted a lease of land on the Dyfi foreshore by the Board of Trade.[21] It was on the north bank near Trefri and since the lease provided for a levy of one penny per ton of slate shipped it seems that he intended to build a pier or jetty on the site. In the following year he bought the forty-three ton smack *Seven Brothers,* a small coastal trader which worked between its home port of Aberdyfi and havens on both sides of the Irish Sea. Just why he wanted a private wharf is not clear, especially as it was further

[18] NLW Machynlleth Deeds, Box 21.
[19] UCNW Mss. 24524.
[20] PRO BT31/881/923c, Resolutions of the Aberdovey Slate Company Limited, 26 November 1867 and 6 October 1869.
[21] PRO MT/68H.33/1869.

from Tywyn than Aberdyfi. Perhaps he objected to the dues, in fact in 1881 W. H. McConnel had a dispute with the Cambrian Railway, who owned Aberdyfi pier and levied two pence per ton of slate shipped, over payments due. He claimed that harbour dues were the responsibility of the master of the vessel, although he agreed to pay in the end.[22] McConnel never built his wharf and in 1888 he was seven months in arrears with the rent for the foreshore lease!

T. H. McConnel suffered from poor health and died from consumption at Dane Bank, Congleton, where he had gone to convalesce, on 13 October 1873.[23] His place as Managing Director was taken by his brother William, who retired from the McConnel and Kennedy business in 1878.

By 1870 production at the quarry had reached 500 tons per month and peaked at just under 8,000 tons per annum in 1877. But this was not enough to bring an adequate return since the undertaking was so heavily over-capitalised, and the Company decided to increase production still further. By then however, they were embroiled in a dispute with the Bryneglwys landlord. On 5 April 1875 the estate's solicitors, Howell and Morgan wrote:

> Mr. Lewis Morris requests your company to desist from using his land for the purpose of working any other quarry than that included in the Bryneglwys lease and requires compensation for the damage already done . . .

The substance of Morris's complaint was that they had diverted water from the Llaeron brook on his land to work the mill on Cantrybedd, driven levels from his land into workings on Hendrewallog and Cantrybedd and tipped waste rock from Hendrewallog onto Bryneglwys land. He was the son of the late Lewis Morris who had granted the 1844 lease, which it will be recalled stipulated a very modest rent. His action therefore may have been motivated by the hope that he could force the company to renegotiate the terms. The company sought advice from Morgan Lloyd, Q.C., who said that since the landlord had made no objection to the construction of the reservoirs to collect the stream waters over a period of several years, and had regularly received the rents due, he could not restrain them from continuing to use them. However, he advised the company not to enlarge the reservoir or to build new ones, and they should stop depositing rubbish from other lands onto Bryneglwys. The lease allowed them to make railways for carrying slate and they were entitled to use them to carry slates from adjoining properties.

The company was in an awkward position since it wanted to enlarge water storage capacity and open up new workings on the Broad Vein. For this they needed to renegotiate the Bryneglwys lease which was due to expire in 1894, and extend it to 1910 in line with the Cantrybedd lease. Their approach to the landlord was met with a response demanding such excssive terms, as might have been expected, as to draw the comment from Morgan Lloyd that 'Lewis Morris is not an accomodating person'. He wanted a minimum rent of £500 for the slate quarry and £200 for the farm! After lengthy negotiations a

[22] NLW Machynlleth Deeds, Box 4.
[23] *Cambrian News*, 17 October 1873.

proposal for an extension of the lease was agreed in December 1877 between Morris and William McConnel, who wrote:

> Mr. Morris has been led lately to change his views as to the future value of his property. He has become aware that after 1894 the company can not only work Cantrybedd and Hendrewallog without his assistance, but they can also — if they are driven to it — make his quarry useless to him, for unless he takes his (slate) blocks over the hill to the Dovey Valley, he will have no other way of getting them to market except with the consent of the company . . . (this was a reference to the freehold tramway linking the quarry to the Talyllyn Railway.)

There were still legal obstacles to be overcome. The will of Lewis Morris senior, the original lessor of 1844, contained no power to accept surrender of leases in possession so an application had to be made to the Chancery Division under the Settled Estates Act, 1877. An order in favour of the petitioners was granted in July 1878, the new lease running for thirty-two years from 31 March 1878. The terms were £40 per annum plus one-fifteenth royalty, subject to a minimum of £100 up to 30 September 1894 and thereafter the same royalty with a £140 minimum. The farm and mineral leases were renewed on the same terms as the originals of 1866.[24]

By 1879 the Company knew that the quarry was never likely to make a profit and McConnel wrote that too much capital had been laid out 'and the shareholders have never had a penny dividend since the commencement'. It was put up for auction on 9 October 1879 at the Queens Hotel, Chester, but no purchaser came forward.[25] There was a severe trade depression at the time and the Company carried on until 16 March 1881 when it was offered for sale again by the same autioneers but at the Mitre Hotel, Manchester. This time it was bought by William McConnel himself for £18,000 plus loose stocks and stores at valuation.[26] An Extraordinary General Meeting of the Abergynolwyn Slate Company Limited on 14 March 1882 resolved to wind up the company and appoint a liquidator.[27]

Now that the burden of over-capitalisation was removed the quarry could be operated profitably and McConnel set about opening new workings on the Broad Vein and building a new mill. Though he was over seventy he remained firmly in control, but he brought in his son William Houldsworth McConnel to assist and eventually to assume control himself. Together they ran the quarry as a family business, though William senior wrote 'the venture on my part is a very bold one for the losses of the quarry hitherto have been enormous and most of my friends think me very foolish in having anything more to do with it.'

In August 1880 a violent storm hit Cardigan Bay and a landslide fell into the Llaeron Reservoir, causing a tidal wave to surge over the dam, taking the top of the dam with it. A torrent of water, turning to liquid mud as it flowed,

[24] NLW Machynlleth Deeds, Box 2.
[25] NLW Sale Catalogues (Merioneth), No. 3 of 1879.
[26] *Mining Journal,* 26 March 1881, p. 379.
[27] *London Gazette,* 14 March 1882, p. 1144-5 and 7 November 1882, p. 4943.

swept down towards Abergynolwyn causing considerable damage — 'it entered the quarry shafts, out of which it drove the air with the force and sound of many cannons'.[28] Fortunately it was Saturday afternoon and the quarrymen were not at work.

In 1889 the working week was changed to five days, Saturday being free so that the men could tend their allotments. They worked ten hours each day, starting at 7 a.m. and finishing at 5.30 p.m., with half an hour for dinner. Previously they had worked 55 hours per week of six days, and wage rates were adjusted so that earnings per week were not significantly lower than before the change.

By 1883 output had climbed to just short of 8,000 tons again, but by 1892 decline to half that figure. From then until 1905 it averaged around 5,500 tons per annum. This picture mirrors the general pattern in the slate industry, caused by a depression in the building trade during the '80s, though this was partly offset by exports. After 1890 the building trade recovered, with domestic (slum clearance) and municipal work, but from 1906 there was intense competition from imported slates and manufactured tiles. When the Penrhyn Quarries, which normally accounted for about a quarter of the North Wales slate output had a three year stoppage, other quarries benefited and these were good years for Bryneglwys.

William McConnel died aged ninety-three on 10 October 1902 after nearly forty years associated with the quarry. According to the *Cambrian News* obituary notice, he was a very strong personality and followd the working of the undertaking most clearly until he end of his life. He was a typical Victorian entrepreneur and fought vigourously for what he belived in. He had the reputation of being a good master, by the standards of the age, he was a paternalistic employer and he usually kept his lawyers busy. He had other business interests besides Bryneglwys, including ironworks in Deeside and coal mines in Derbyshire. He died at Knockdolian Mansion, Colmonell, Ayrshire.[29]

By the closing years of the McConnel leases the best rock had been extracted and the only way to maintain production would have been to extend the underground workings westward on Cantrybedd. Apart from the capital investment required, working costs would increase bcause the blocks and rubbish would have to be transported over greater distances, to reach the mill and tips. W. H. McConnel wrote to G. R. G. Pughe in 1901, saying that in considering forward work he didn't wish to invest further capital since it would not bring sufficient profit before the leases expired. It cost from £600 to £800 to open a new chamber and he offered Pughe the chance to invest new capital in the undertaking himself. Not surprisingly Pughe declined, so McConnel replied that he would run production down to the level of the dead rent.[30]

So McConnel decided to cut as much rock as possible from the walls between the chambers to the point where the roofs were in danger of collapsing, an all

[28] *Cambrian News,* 13 August 1880.
[29] *Cambrian News,* 17 October 1902.
[30] UCNW Mss. 24524.

too common practice in quarries starved of development funds. The Cantrybedd leases were due to expire in 1907 and 1909, and on 30 November 1908 they were extended, one of them in retrospect, to expire on 31 March 1910 bringing them into line with the Bryneglwys leases. McConnel decided to stop cutting new rock in December 1909 to allow time for the business to be wound up. His Managing Director R. B. Yates and the Agent, Meyrick Roberts tried unsuccessfully to negotiate extensions to the leases and on 17 December 1909 Meyrick Roberts read a notice to the men that the quarry would be closed permanently the following day. It was reported that:

> They passed a unanimous vote of thanks to Mr. McConnel for carrying on the quarry for so many years, during which there had been no unpleasantness . . . the best feelings had existed between master and men . . . they regretted very much having lost their old master. Their wish was to finish their lives in his service.[31]

So the heyday of the quarry was over, the best rock was gone and no capital development had occurred for several years. The industry was declining, the number of men employed in North Wales slate quarries falling from 16,766 in 1898 to 13,000 in 1909. It seemed that Bryneglwys — 'the old place' — and the Talyllyn Railway were finished.

As the termination of the lease approached, McConnel had to face allegations from the Cantrybedd landlord that the quarry had not been worked according to the terms of the lease and Pughe called in a surveyor, Thomas Jones, to report on the state of the works. His report dated May 1910 survives and contains a good description of the Cantrybedd quarry as he saw it.[32] He found that the Company had worked away the walls between chambers on three floors, they had caused the collapse of the quarry from chambers 3 to 6, and they had allowed waste rock and water to accumulate in floor 75. Jones believed that McConnel was liable for damages because he had

> not followed and pursued the bed of slate according to the law and custom of slate quarries . . . failed to deliver up the quarries with all pits, shafts, levels, roads . . . in good order and repair.

He thought that the damages would be met, approximately, if McConnel surrendered the whole of the fixed and loose machinery, plant and tramways without compensation therefor. He estimated that these items had cost about £12,000 when installed.

But McConnel was not one to give in easily. His trump card was the freehold tramway which alone connected Pughe's quarry to the outside world and without which it would be worthless. Although Pughe had the right of carriage, McConnel was not obliged to run it, or the Talyllyn Railway either, if he chose not to. This ploy meant that it was pointless for Pughe to take McConnel to court and ensured that the machinery could only be valued on a scrap basis. In the end the value was assessed at £875 and McConnel began clearing stocks of slate and started to dismantle and remove the machinery.

[31] *Cambrian News,* 17 and 24 December 1909.
[32] UCNW Mss. 24524.

Meanwhile there was much concern amongst the quarrymen and their families, especially in Abergynolwyn. A press statement by Yates at the end of December explained that the quarry owners were not willing to renew the leases, though they were prepared to continue working the quarry for a short period subject to certain conditions.[33] Their object in doing so was firstly to give the men employment over the winter months, and secondly in the hope that trade might improve during that time in which case the prospect of a new company being formed would be greater. The landlords, however, could not all agree to this proposal and so the villagers, deprived of their main source of income, had nowhere to turn to in the immediate neighbourhood for work. A few men set to work in a small slate quarry on the Narrow Vein at Rhydyronen, a short distance up the Nant Braich-y-rhiw from the T.R. station. Others drifted further afield, and those remaining appealed to their freshly elected M.P. for help in finding a new owner willing to carry the place on.

In the general election of January 1910 Mr. Henry Haydn Jones had defeated his Conservative opponent to become the new Liberal member for the County of Merioneth. He was a well known Tywyn resident who had served in local government, being at one time chairman of the Finance Committee of the County Council. He was returned unopposed in the General Election of December 1910, and he held the seat until his retirement in 1945.

Haydn Jones's efforts to find a purchaser were unsuccessful, as might have been expected in view of the poor state of the quarry. Eventually, in January 1911 he bought the quarry, village and railway himself for £5,250. His move was precipitated by McConnel's action in removing some of the machinery, but he was not a wealthy man. He had to borrow capital to make the purchase and of course his political popularity was at stake, in view of the large number of quarrymen in his Merioneth constituency. His action led to ecstatic comments in the press, for example:

> Blessings emanated from every mouth on this his latest and best of all efforts to serve his town and country. It is indeed difficult to estimate what a boon he has (at very great cost to himself financially) conferred on the whole district, and nothing but wholehearted thankfulness is heard on all hands . . . the quarry will be worked by a gentleman who knows what it is to do a days work and does it every day, and who will see fair play done to the youngest lad as well as his head manager, etc. . . .[34]

He negotiated with the landowners to set new leases, but G. R. G. Pughe, still smarting from his brush with McConnel, responded with a draft containing such provisions as:

> the lessees to develop the quarry in such a way that there shall be not less than (left blank) chambers in working order at any time after the first seven years, and as soon as one chamber is exhausted a new one is to be opened, and partition walls are not to be worked away . . .

[33] *Cambrian News,* 31 December 1909.
[34] *Cambrian News,* 3 February 1911.

Ellis Davies, Haydn Jones's solicitor, replied offering terms of one twenty-fifth royalty, a dead rent of £50 rising to £100 in the seventh year and a further rent of £12.10.0d. (£12.50) for the buildings, water and land for tipping. The lessor was to be responsible for the cost of his own solicitor. He added:

> Mr. Haydn Jones feels rather strongly that whilst he is incurring very considerable risk for the sake of the industry of the village, the landowners are prepared to take no risk at all, although without the railway their mineral property would of course be valueless.[35]

Pughe was unmoved and on 6 May 1911 Davies wrote asking him if he would be prepared to make an offer for the quarry machinery as Haydn Jones intended to dispose of it and close the railway. As late as 20 October the *Cambrian News* reported that negotiations between the new owner and the ground landlords had proved abortive. Finally, a settlement was announced on 28 October and on the following Monday about twenty men were engaged to undertake preparatory clearing work.[36]

The Abergynolwyn Slate and Slab Company Limited was incorporated on 2 November 1911, its main objects being to purchase the quarry machinery, plant, etc., from Haydn Jones in consideration of 1,500 fully paid up shares of £1 each, and to carry on the business of slate quarrying.[37] Haydn Jones was the sole Director.

The new Cantrybedd lease was for thirty years, from 29 September and 1 December respectively. The royalty on Hendrewallog was one twenty-fifth and the dead rent £10 per annum, compared with one-fifteenth and £50 for the same ground in 1866! The lease allowed the company to divert and make watercourses, to carry waters to other premises, quarries and mines nearby and to deposit rubbish elsewhere than on Hendrewallog — clearly Haydn Jones had done his homework![38]

The new company soon found that the quarry was unlikely ever to bring in a profit because of the lack of development work for many years and the very slack demand for slate. Haydn Jones instituted a system of paying wages fortnightly instead of monthly, and a wage scale which guaranteed a minimum of 4/6d. (22½p) per day for quarrymen and 4/- (20p) for labourers, which was paid even if actual earnings fell below those figures. These rates were somewhat lower, on a week of five days, than those drawn up in a charter by the North Wales Quarrymen's Union in September 1911. By 1913 there were 120 men employed by the Company but then the army took many of the young men during the war, the numbers falling to around forty in 1918.

In September of that year the Union applied to the North Wales Slate Quarry Proprietors Association, on behalf of its members, for new terms of employment. They requested day wage rates of 7/-, 6/6d. and 6/3d. (35p, 32½p and 31p) for

[35] UCNW Mss. 24524.
[36] *Cambrian News,* 3 November 1911.
[37] Companies House file No. 118357, Abergynolwyn Slate and Slab Company Limited.
[38] Copy in possession of H. Jones, Esq., Tywyn.

skilled quarrymen, rock labourers and labourers respectively and that letting standards for bargains should be set at 1/- (5p) above day rates. They also proposed a sliding scale to allow for variations in the prices of slates, day rates to be raised or lowered by 6d. (2½p) for each 10 per cent change up or down in the official price. Wages were to be paid weekly instead of at the end of each quarry month (four week period).

The North Wales Quarrymen's Union had been founded in 1874. After achieving early success, they claimed eighty members at Bryneglwys by 1878, that is 30 per cent of the men employed. In later years the Union failed to establish itself as an effective negotiating body and suffered a severe setback after the bitter disputes at the Penrhyn Quarries, Bethesda, in 1896-7 and 1900-03. Following the appointment of Robert Thomas Jones of Blaenau Ffestiniog as general secretary in 1909, membership increased substantially and the internal organisation of the Union was centralised and strengthened. R. T. Jones became the Labour M.P. for Caernarfon from 1922-3 and he remained N.W.Q.U. general secretary until the merger of the Union with the T.G.W.U. in 1927.[39]

In 1917 the North Wales Slate Quarry Proprietors Association was formed and they recognised the Union as a negotiating body. By 1918 two-thirds of the men at Bryneglwys were Union members and on 10 September R. T. Jones wrote a letter to Haydn Jones which was the opening shot in a campaign that led to some very acrimonious exchanges between the two men. He wrote, on behalf of the Union's members at Bryneglwys, requesting the same terms as those in its application to the Proprietors Association. In addition they requested an increase in the working week from five to six days by the addition of Saturday morning working.[40]

Haydn Jones was not a member of the Proprietors Association and he certainly regarded conditions at the quarry as a private matter between himself and the men. His reply was marked 'confidential' and sought Jones's views 'as a friend's advice to a friend in difficulty'. He said that if the requests were seriously meant then he would have to close the quarry at once.

> . . . My position is a simple one. I restarted the quarry to provide work for the men who were unemployed. I have paid them as you know a minimum wage all along, when other quarries did nothing of the kind and if I could I would, without being asked, gladly increase the minimum because I believe the best work is to be got from men who are decently paid.
>
> I have carried the place entirely on borrowed capital and in the interests of the men and by so doing I have increased my overdrafts by many thousands of £'s. This increase is the loss I have sustained in trying to keep the men employed and an industry alive.
>
> And what is the position today? The army has taken the young men. Men who went on their knees to ask me to reopen the quarry have left for temporary employment at ridiculous wages in the timber trade, and I have been left with a little over forty men, mostly old, infirm and long past their best, and a few young lads over 14.

[39] Merfyn Jones, *The North Wales Quarrymen's Union.*
[40] CRO XNWQU/184.

> And now you come along and ask me to do the impossible. I have lost thousands of £'s already and as I explained to the men a few months ago, I can make a pile of money now by scrapping the machinery and especially the railway.
>
> No business can be run for long except at a profit. I have run the quarry for 7 years at a big loss in the hope of getting it refunded if better times come. But to carry it on and pay what you suggest, much as I would like to do so, is simply impossible and I write quite frankly to say that if your letter is seriously meant, I shall at once take steps to close down and realise my losses by scrapping the Railway while it is possible to get big prices for the rails. Or in the alternative I am quite willing to sell the whole concern at a valuation to anyone who can carry the old place on and pay the wages your Union demands.
>
> I hope you understand the position. If the place could be made to pay the wages you set forth, I would be the first man to agree to do so — indeed you should never have had an opportunity of asking me to do it — I would have done it of my own accord. I have Old Age Pensioners at work here — who in the name of fortune culd make enough money to pay those 6/3 per day?
>
> Quite recently I had an interview with a number of quarrymen. I showed them my bank account from the outset. They saw how my overdrafts had increased by thousands and I gave them the option of continuing or closing down the place. I do not feel justified in completely ruining my circumstances in the interests of other people and I shall be glad to learn of anyone who has sacrificed more for others. If you seriously mean to ask me to do the impossible I shall have no alternative but to close down and that of course would be by far the best course for me.
>
> Let me have your views.

R. T. Jones replied asking for an answer which he could submit to his executive. Haydn Jones said that his letter was confidential and must remain so, and that he would make no formal reply for the moment other than an acknowledgement. He would await the result of the meeting with th Proprietors Association and after that he would lay the circumstances before the men at the quarry. They would decide whether to go on or to have the place closed.

Jones replied bluntly that if the men were approached in that way it would mean that Haydn Jones was diregarding the Union the men belonged to and the Society authorised to act on their behalf. The Union made the application and they should settle, according to the opinion of the men and as far as it was fair to other quarries.

In October 1918 the Union reached agreement with the Proprietors Association and they applied for the same terms at Bryneglwys. Haydn Jones reiterated the reasons for his inability to meet the terms. To do what he had done, he had realised effects and sold a plantation of timber. He had offered to close down so that the men might accept better paid work in the neighbourhood, and he had no wish to keep them if they could do better elsewhere.

The Union was not satisfied, and R. T. Jones wrote:

> . . . It appears as if you were trying to put the blame on the Union for stopping the quarry, and as no other permanent employment was available, you were taking advantage of that fact to refuse to discuss our application.
>
> We have a fair idea as to the depression in the slate trade for the last

> few years but we know substantial improvement has taken place lately. This was acknowledged by the Proprietors Association when they agreed on improved terms, and we cannot understand why your position should be worse than some of them, if not all.
>
> You state that the quarries are exhausted, which means that no development is taking place so the cost of working cannot be high proportionately if we assume you are working solely on producing rock without developing. We are given to understand your slates are sold at a lower price than the authorised Price List of the Proprietors Association. If so we submit that is at the expense of the employees and its influence must be to lower the standard in all North Wales Quarries.
>
> We note your remarks about the losses you have incurred in the quarry. We cannot disprove this but suggest that we be allowed to appoint a qualified person to inspect the books as they affect the quarry only apart from your other concerns.
>
> You may rest assured that we shall consult the men and it is they who have to decide eventually and your position will be explained to them as well as we can. We hope you will not take up the uncompromising attitude we feel you take, but that you will meet us to discuss whether we cannot arrive at an amicable understanding.

This was too much for Haydn Jones. He released his fury in a letter on 10 December:

> . . . the assertion that I am trying to put the blame on the Union for stopping the quarry is absolutely untrue. It would be well if before making such an accusation you acquainted yourself with the facts. Months before the men joined the Union, I showed them my bank book. I disclosed everything to them and offered to close the quarry for the duration of the war so that they could take timber felling work at high wages. I undertook to reopen when the timber felling ceased . . . The exhaustion of the quarry is not due to lack of development. As a practical quarryman you must know that there are quarries which no amount of expenditure will make successful. I was well aware of this at Abergynolwyn and it was at the urgent appeal of the men that I undertook to reopen the quarry for the sole purpose of providing work for the men at a time of great depression, guaranteeing a minimum wage and as a result I have incurred serious loss to myself.
>
> The suggestion that the slates are sold under the market value is absolutely peurile. Do you allege that I am stupid enough to sell the produce at a lower price than it will command?
>
> But the most amazing request of all is that I should allow my books to be examined by a 'qualified person'! . . . But as I have nothing to conceal, I am quite prepared to produce my bank book and give either yourself or Mr. Joseph Williams (the N.W.Q.U. Merioneth Organiser) any other information necessary. To an ousider I will not . . . I have placed to the credit of the quarry several thousand pounds of private capital upon which not a penny interest has been paid! In addition a sum of between two and three thousand pounds has been realised for timber sold off the estate, all this has been used to carry the place on, the rents of the Abergynolwyn houses have also been thrown in! When you examine my accounts you will see how hopelessly you have been misled . . .

A meeting was arranged at the quarry to enable the Union party, consisting of R. T. Jones and Joseph Williams to discuss the books with the Manager, David

Jones. Some notes taken by the Union party show that there were on average fifty men employed, paid fortnightly. Bargainers, that is men paid under contract, made 5/- (25p) per day minimum and contract labourers 4/6d. (22½p). A joiner (old man), a smith (not trained) and a craneman received 4/6d., a saw sharpener (consumptive) 4/- (20p). They estimated that an increase in all the men's wages of 1/- (5p) a day would cost the Company £60 extra per month. David Jones later wrote to R. T. Jones enclosing a copy of the 'make' of slates for two four-week periods in 1918 and 1919. Very few slates were best quality, the total value of best and medium being £344 and £222 for the two periods respectively. He added:

> I do not believe it is worth for you to trouble much about the make, because Mr. Haydn Jones has already decided what course to be taken with regard to the quarry, which course I am sorry to say will cause a great loss to the people of Abergynolwyn and all the neighbourhood.

The Union were now left in no doubt that the finances of Bryneglwys Quarry were indeed as shaky as Haydn Jones had told them. Their only realistic option was to retreat, at least for the time being. R. T. Jones accordingly wrote to Haydn Jones on 17 February 1919:

> . . . I am instructed to state that this application forwarded by us shall not be pressed until such time as we feel the state of affairs will improve . . .

Haydn Jones thus won the first battle. When trade did pick up a few months later he advanced wages by 2/- (10p) per day, without of course consulting the Union. But there had been severe inflation in that year, and higher rates had been agreed with the Proprietors Association already, so in July they applied for the same working hours, including Saturdays and the same bonus rates as those agreed with the Association. R. T. Jones was not amused by Haydn Jones's reply that there was no objection to shorter hours and Saturday working, provided hat there was a corresponding revision of wage rates! His letter was dated 5 August 1919:

> . . . I am istructed to say that you did not let us know about the increases in wage rates at your quarry, although our members told us. In view of our decision to advise the men to carry on pending improvement in output &c we surely had a right to notification from you. It appears to us you tried to convey to the men 'that the Trade Union could not be of any good to them'. We do not believe this was your idea but the methods adopted would carry that impression . . . My Executive agrees 'it now remains for the men to decide' and I am instructed to take their views, which I hope to do about the end of the month and I shall explain to them fully and fairly the position taken by you, so that they can know the whole facts before coming to a decision, which we shall convey to you at once . . .

At the time of this acrimonious correspondence there was, inevitably, a growing tension within the quarry Some feared for the loss of their livelihood, particularly the older men, if Haydn Jones decided to cut his losses and close the business. The younger, more militant element were accused of political agitation aimed at embarassing Haydn Jones. Matters came to a head when the secretary of the local Union Lodge, Griffith Griffiths, alleged that he had been suspended by the manager because of his Union activities. It is impossible to discover the full facts of the case at this distance of time, but Griffiths wrote to R. T. Jones on 2 August:

> . . . they have not thrown me out but they have stopped the work in that particular part where I was working, though there are some apprentices still working there. I asked them a plain question — were you stopping me because of the Union? He never said yes and he never said no and then I asked if I would get my work back when the place was ready for working again, but he didn't bind himself one way or the other. What he wants is for me to go there and ask for work and he would give me terms, that no mention be made of the Union in the quarry. That's how he deals with people. He said he would send for me when he wanted me. I could be here for six weeks easily and this is my difficulty now. If I go to work somewhere else, that will be enough excuse for him to say that he did not stop me and he could give my place to somebody else, but I must look for something next week, I can't wait any longer . . . The Quarrymen's Union is too weak to defend the workers who have to work for five days a week for seven shillings wages . . . (The original letter is in Welsh).

Clearly the Manager had decided to suspend Griffiths, regarding him as an agitator, in the hope that he would be forced to find work somewhere else. R. T. Jones took the matter up by adding in his letter to Haydn Jones on 5 August:

> . . . I understand that our local secretary has been out of work the last fortnight and it seems he is being penalised for being a member of our Union. I understand that he has been warned about what happened at Bethesda, which we take to mean refers to the men who failed to get back to the Penrhyn Quarries after the last strike. I bring this to your notice without comment at the moment and trust that no further action will be necessary.

This was of course a red flag to a bull and Haydn Jones's reply was a diatribe:

> . . . The increase (in wages) was paid not as a result of representations by your Union, but by better working results and prices. I simply paid them a higher rate the moment I was able to do so. If you suggest that I must do nothing directly with those whom I employ — many of whom are not members of your Union — I am afraid I shall never be able to agree to such a proposal . . . It has been apparent for some time that the chamber worked by your secretary's crew would have to be stopped in order that miners might open it afresh. You secretary's partners insisted on stopping at the end of the last quarry month although the manager wished them to carry on another fortnight. He knew perfectly well and to allege discrimination is as wicked as it is unfounded. You say that you 'trust no further action will be necessary'. If that is intended to intimidate me, and it can have no other meaning, you have for once committed a grievous mistake. You cannot intimidate a man who has sacrificed so much for the men and who is quite prepared to close down any moment the men think fit to say so. Why should I carry on and put up with wilful misrepresentation such as this? Let me tell you quite frankly that you are at liberty to take whatever action you think fit. When you take action, I too will make known to the public how in spite of bad timekeeping, refusing to pay the quarry rates

> of pay to journeymen, declining to employ rubbishers or apprentices, consistently refusing to work underground to assist his partners when necessary, as well as other irregularities which in his interests I refrain for the moment from specifying — I kept your secretary till his chamber had to be stopped for development. Had I done my duty by the quarry the man would have been dismissed long ago and he is one of those who begged me to start the place afresh and he undertook to exert himself to the utmost to make the venture a success. But I retained him and it was my intention to take him back as well as all his partners, the moment the chamber was ready. But now that you have threatened me, I am certainly not prepared to do so without fully considering what this may mean. Please take the action you allude to, whatever that may be. I am not going to be dictated to nor intimidated when all I am doing is done in the intrests of the men . . .

Joseph Williams went to Abergynolwyn and tried to make an appointment with the manager to discuss the treatment of Griffiths so that he could report back to the Executive Committee, allowing them to come to a 'conclusion that would be fair to both sides'. David Jones gave him short shrift:

> . . . I am sorry to say that I have to inform you that I am not in any way going to argue with you my doings at the quarry on the evidence of a man like Griffith Griffiths.

As a result of these events R. T. Jones wrote to Haydn Jones pointing out that he had made serious allegations against Griffiths, yet his case was not being fairly heard:

> . . . Mr. Joseph Williams went to Abergynolwyn to investigate and I have his report. Your manager refused to see him to discuss the matter and this weakens your case considerably. There is one fact of which you may be unaware which if true makes your statement about stopping the chamber being the reason for stopping Griffiths appear like a half-truth (presumably Williams's report that other men were making slates from rock obtained from Griffiths' chamber). I suggest that you investigate further, your honour as a man demands it. The new accusations against Griffiths are serious and he should have the opportunity to defend himself. According to our information he is unjustly accused and treated, judged and condemned on inaccurate and one-sided evidence . . .

Haydn Jones simply repeated the charges, alleging that his manager knew the incident was an attempt to cause trouble. He went on:

> . . . I again say that I have done all I can for the men at enormous loss to myself and in the face of much ingratitude. If the men think I am not doing all I can for them, well the sooner they tell me the better. Of one thing I am certain, I will not go under present conditions. I have told this to one of the oldrest workmen yesterday and I must have an immediate decision. To lose money helping others is sufficient. To be wilfully misrepresented and disbelieved is intolerable.

R. T. Jones retorted that it was pointless to continue the correspondence on these lines. Arrangements were made to determine the men's views on whether or not the quarry would continue. Attitudes amongst the men were hardening — Griffiths wrote that there was opposition to the Union which had taken a

A group of quarrymen posed in front of the Old Mill before the First World War.
(Gwynedd Archives Service)

Another group outside the Old Mill. Mr. Griffith Evans, blacksmith at the quarry from 1921, has identified the following by **name:** back row, left to right, Evan J. Rowlands, David Rowlands, unknown, Owen Jones, Evan Humphries, unknown, Evan Owen, unknown, John D. Rowlands, Dafydd Humphries. Seated, l. to r., John Griffiths, Ellis O. Ellis, Lewis Edwards, unknown, William Owen (standing, hand on kettle), William H. Williams, Daniel Lewis, John Meredith Jones. The boy in front is possibly Thomas Jones **(Pandy)**, son of Owen Jones.

(Caradog Jones collection)

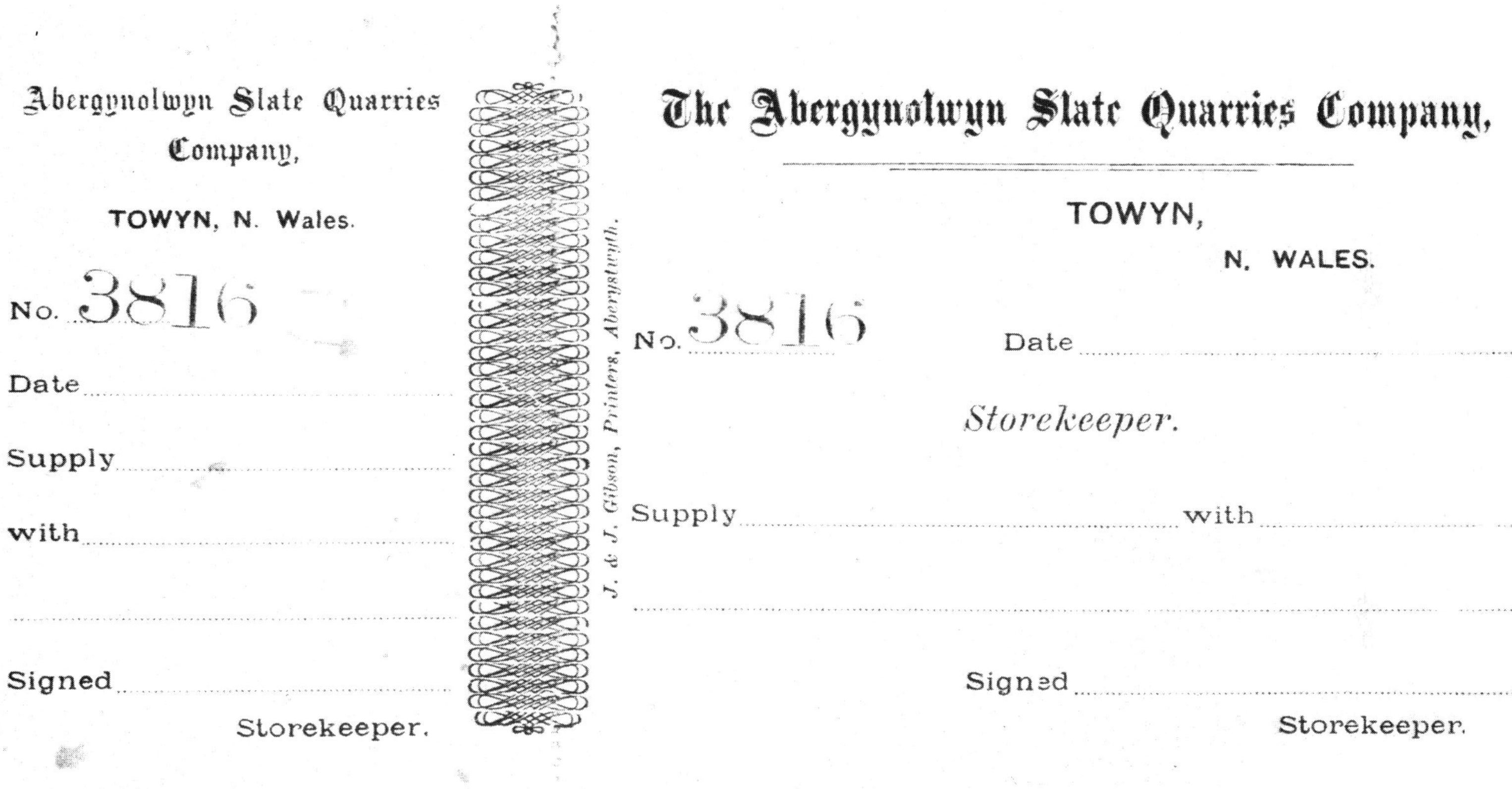
Abergynolwyn Slate Quarries Company,

TOWYN, N. Wales.

No. 3816

Date

Supply

with

Signed

Storekeeper.

J. & J. Gibson, Printers, Aberystwyth.

The Abergynolwyn Slate Quarries Company,

TOWYN,

N. WALES.

No. 3816 Date

Storekeeper.

Supply with

Signed

Storekeeper.

Requisition slip of the Abergynolwyn Slate Quarries Co.

(O. H. Prosser)

The Abergynolwyn Slate & Slab Company, Ltd. M 90.

Loading Station:
TOWYN, Cambrian Railways.

Prices and Particulars of Blue Slates from their Bryneglwys and Cantrybedd Quarries, Abergynolwyn.

Shipping Port:
ABERDOVEY

Best (1st Quality).			Best Mediums & Mediums.			Covering Capacity per M. of 1,200 with 3in. lap.	Seconds.		
Sizes.	Computed Weight per M. of 1,200.	Price per M. of 1,200.	Sizes.	Computed Weight per M. of 1,200.	Price per M. of 1,200.		Sizes.	Computed Weight per M. of 1,200.	Price per M. of 1,200.
In. In.	Cwts.	£ s. d.	In. In.	Cwts.	£ s. d.	Sq. Yards.	In. In.	Cwts.	£ s. d.
24 by 14	68	31 7 6	24 by 14	73	33 7 6	136	24 by 14	90	25 7 6
24 ,, 12	58	30 12 6	24 ,, 12	63	29 10 0	117	24 ,, 12	84	22 12 6
22 ,, 12	53	24 5 0	22 ,, 12	58	23 12 6	106	22 ,, 12	73	18 5 0
22 ,, 11	48	22 5 0	22 ,, 11	53	21 15 0	97	22 ,, 11	63	16 10 0
20 ,, 12	48	21 15 0	20 ,, 12	53	21 7 6	95	20 ,, 12	65	16 0 0
20 ,, 10	38	19 12 6	20 ,, 10	43	18 12 6	78	20 ,, 10	54	14 7 6
18 ,, 10	34	15 2 6	18 ,, 10	39	14 15 0	70	18 ,, 10	48	10 17 6
18 ,, 9	31	12 12 6	18 ,, 9	35	12 0 0	62	18 ,, 9	42	8 15 0
16 ,, 10	29	11 12 6	16 ,, 10	35	11 5 0	60	16 ,, 10	42	8 5 0
16 ,, 9	27	10 5 0	16 ,, 9	31	9 17 6	54	16 ,, 9	34	7 7 6
16 ,, 8	24	9 2 6	16 ,, 8	28	8 15 0	48	16 ,, 8	32	6 7 6
14 ,, 10	26	9 2 6	14 ,, 10	30	8 15 0	51	14 ,, 10	37	6 15 0
14 ,, 9	24	8 1 6	14 ,, 9	27	7 15 0	46	14 ,, 9	32	5 19 0
4 ,, 8	22	7 0 0	14 ,, 8	24	6 15 0	41	14 ,, 8	27	5 2 6
14 ,, 7	20	6 7 6	14 ,, 7	21	6 2 6	37	14 ,, 7	24	5 0 0
13 ,, 7	18	5 0 0	13 ,, 7	19	4 10 0	32	13 ,, 7	21	3 7 6
12 ,, 10	23	6 7 6	12 ,, 10	24	6 0 0	42	12 ,, 10	26	4 10 0
12 ,, 9	21	5 14 0	12 ,, 9	23	5 7 6	38	12 ,, 9	24	4 1 6
12 ,, 8	20	5 0 0	12 ,, 8	21	4 15 0	33	12 ,, 8	23	3 12 6
12 ,, 6	15	3 15 0	12 ,, 6	16	3 7 6	25	12 ,, 6	18	2 17 6
10 ,, 8	16	3 17 6	10 ,, 8	17	3 10 0	26	10 ,, 8	19	2 15 0
10 ,, 6	12	2 5 0	10 ,, 6	13	2 2 6	20	10 ,, 6	15	1 12 6

ON WAR OFFICE AND ADMIRALTY LISTS.

Price Card of the Abergynolwyn Slate and Slab Co. Ltd.
(Gwynedd Archives Service)

"VAENGALED" Welsh Grey Slates

Stand in a class of their own, and combine the **three prime essentials** of the

IDEAL ROOF COVERING, *viz.* :

DURABILITY.—No atmosphere, however acid-laden, will impair them.

ARTISTIC APPEARANCE.—Their colour, thickness and rough texture do away with the flat, monotonous effect of the usual slated roof.

LOW COST.—Once on the roof, nothing but an accident will necessitate renewal.

N.B.—In order to avoid the substitution of inferior Slates, Architects are respectfully requested to specify "VAENGALED" WELSH GREY Slates from the Abergynolwyn Slate and Slab Co., Ltd.

A few of the numerous important buildings on which "Vaengaled' Slates have been used :—

Westminster Hall (Star Chamber Court Side).
Goldsborough Hall (Princess Mary's Residence). Additions.
St. Edmunds Church, Tycroes, Carmarthen.
Sherborne Hospital, Durham.
National Library of Wales, Aberystwyth.
Kirk Braddon Church, Isle-of-Man.
King Edward VII. Sanatorium, Talgarth.
St. David's Hotel, Harlech.
Waifs and Strays Home, Darlington.
Memorial Hospital, Towyn.
Hawarden Castle Estate.
Marquis of Anglesey's Estate.
Silver Stand, Racecourse, York.
Buildings on Doncaster Race Course.
Waterworks Offices and Depot, Edmund Road, Sheffield.
Barnsley Road Schools, Sheffield.
Garden Cities and Housing Schemes in different parts of the Country
Etc. Etc. Etc.

Extract from price card of 'Vaengaled' slates. Issued in 1925, this was part of a sales drive to promote Broad Vein slates.
(R. H. Jones collection)

Group at Bryneglwys including Griffith Griffiths, the local NWQU secretary, second from the left behind the boy in the front row; R. O. Williams who later became the Agent is the clean-shaven figure standing fourth from the right in the same row as Griffiths. Some of the others also appear in the previous picture, taken a dozen years or so earlier.

(Gwynedd Archives Service)

A group at the quarry c. 1930. From left to right, Hugh Griffiths, Ieuan Davies, Iorweth Owen, Islwyn Evans.

(Gwynedd Archives Service)

Another group at the same period. From the left, Iorweth Owen, Caradog Jones, John Owen Jones, John William Jones, Walter Davies (with splitting chisel), David John Jones, John Jones.

(Gwynedd Archives Service)

public form. The threat of closure was now quite open and all sorts of rumours were rife. He believed that Haydn Jones meant to keep the quarry going with non-Union labour.

By mid-January 1920 Haydn Jones issued an ultimatum giving fourteen days for the men to decide whether to carry on or let him close the quarry. On 27 January R. T. Jones informed him that:

> Our members at your quarry met to discuss your statement submitted to them on 20 January and came to the following decision: Last Thursday evening, the Union Lodge met to consider our position, and considering that Mr. Haydn Jones was intent on closing the quarry, and saying absolutely positively that he was going to, it was unanimously passed that it would be unwise to push things that far.
>
> Signed by the three local officials.
>
> (The original resolution is in Welsh)

This did not satisfy Haydn Jones, who received no further notification from the men and accordingly closed the quarry as from 31 January 1920. He did not make any move to dispose of the machinery or take advantage of the 'big prices' for rails. A newspaper interview was published about a fortnight later.[41] The reporter stated that there was an impression in the district that the trouble had been fostered by malcontents trying to make political capital against Haydn Jones as member for the County. He expressed the hope that the wiser heads amongst the men would be able to tame the wilder spirits and bring reason to bear on outside agencies (i.e. the Union). Haydn Jones wrote a long letter on 1 March which was duly published. He recounted the history of his associaion with the quarry and his inability to meet the demands of the Union, and prophesied dire consequences if highter wages were to be granted to all quarrymen. He also stated, characteristically, that 'the public have now been furnished with an accurate account of the affair.'[42] Our search has failed to reveal an account furnished to the public giving the men's point of view!

Haydn Jones's closure of the quarry effectively called the men's bluff. Whilst it was one thing for the Union to agree, however grudgingly, to carry on working at wage rates below the norm, it was out of the question for them to ask him to re-open on the same terms. R. T. Jones had been careful not to associate his executive with the decision of the local lodge when he sent their resolution to Haydn Jones.

A month after the closure, under pressure particularly from the older men, the Lodge decided to appeal to R. T. Jones to meet Haydn Jones to discuss re-opening the quarry. Besides the hardship of having no income, they were anxious lest the machinery might soon be sold off, and they wrote:

> . . . let us know if you please if there is any difficulty for you to accede to our plan, and that soon because we can't wait much longer.

The reply was dated 3 March, and Jones explained at length his view of the situation. He said he would be criticised by some for not calling them out on

[41] *Cambrian News,* 13 February 1920.
[42] *Cambrian News,* 5 March 1920.

strike, which some members had wanted. Because he knew that there was no alternative work available at Abergynolwyn if Bryneglwys stopped he had persuaded the executive to agree to the quarry being worked at lower wages and longer hours than any other in the County. In any case a ballot, with three-quarters in favour, would have been necessary before calling the men out. He went on:

> . . . If I had the will I do not have the authority to send to Mr. Haydn Jones asking him to open discussions on the question of re-opening the quarry on the same terms — worse terms than in any other quarry, and I have no reason to believe that the Executive Council would give me authority to do that . . .

He added that a false report had appeared in a newspaper saying that the Union had asked the Agent to re-open the quarry on the same terms. They had done no such thing, and he had seen another report that Haydn Jones had just re-opened on the same terms. The only way that the Executive were likely to agree to start new discussions would be on the same terms as in the other quarries . . . 'I do not think Mr. Haydn Jones would be prepared to do that.'

By the time that letter had reached Abergynolwyn the quarry had indeed re-opened on the same terms as before and with a new Manager, R. O. Williams. So ended the involmement of the Union, at least at National level, in the affairs of Bryneglwys Quarry.

The post-war boom in housebuilding and the consequent demand for slate helped to boost employment in the industry and by the mid-twenties over 150 men worked at Bryneglwys. Air compressors driven by water wheels were installed on both veins so that powered rock drills at last began to replace the old hand drill. Fresh attempts to market the Broad Vein slates reflected McConnel's efforts of forty years earlier, one customer being supplied for roofing Westminster Hall, but the boom was short-lived and in the 1930s the number employed fell to around sixty.

The quarry and the Talyllyn Railway were by then suffering from accumulated arrears of maintenance after many years of neglect and they sank into a decline from which there could be no recovery. This was accompanied by an obscurity only occasionally relieved by such mentions in the press as for example in 1937 when it was announced that the quarrymen were granted leave for the August Bank Holiday Week on full pay to attend the National Eisteddfod at Machynlleth, or double pay for those electing to work instead. The following year it was unanimously resolved that a small donation be deducted from the men's wages each month for the Barnardo's Homes, following a visit by one of their representatives.

A more ominous report appeared in December 1939:

> A few minutes before workmen entered the underground chamber of Bryneglwys . . . the roof of one chamber fell in and the nearby river broke its bank and flooded a section of the quarry. Soon other parts fell in, including a large area of mountain.[43]

[43] *Quarry Managers Journal,* Vol. 22, January 1940, p. 309.

Mr. Caradog Jones remembered this incident in more detail:

> Between every chamber and the next there was a ten yard pillar holding the roof up. You couldn't reach the roof — it had gone too high — and they started working on these pillars. People in, say chamber No. 10, were working on the pillar one side and people were working in No. 11 on the other side, so the pillar was getting weaker with the result that it caved in. I remember quite well I was working up there in No. 9 and we knew there was something wrong. There was a 'bounce' in the rock and a small piece of rock came down so we had to listen carefully. We were building a wall right across a big fall and we finished everything by Friday afternoon. When we arrived there on the Monday morning after, the chamber caved in, before we went in. All the tools, crane, ladders and everything were buried underneath and it was a great loss to the quarry because it was a very good chamber. We could work up to a thousand slates a day in the best part of it and I mean not small ones but the most marketable — countess (20×10) and duchess (24×12). We did it without killing ourselves. Well, when it caved in I remember the manager coming to talk with us and he was sorry he stopped us. There was nowhere else to go, so home we went.

In the war years a dozen or so men carried on, only five remaining at the end in 1946. Production in the final year amounted to 88 tons of roofing and damp course slate. After remaining stocks of slates were removed the quarry was abandoned, the machinery and plant being left *in situ* until 1952 when they were taken for scrap by Williams of Harlech.

Sir Henry Haydn Jones — he was knighted in the Coronation Honours List of May 1937, for public and political services — died aged eighty-six on 2 July 1950. He served as Liberal M.P. for Merioneth until 1945 when he retired, not contesting the election of that year. Like William McConnel, he kept the wheels turning for the last forty-odd years of his long life, latterly on the Talyllyn Railway alone which lingered in an advanced state of decrepitude after the quarry closure in 1947. He had purchased the Aberllefenni Slate quarry lease in 1935, and the Abergynolwyn Slate and Slab Company became Aberllefenni Slate Quarries Limited from 1956, a company which is still trading, the ultimate holding concern being the Bow Slate and Enamel Company.

Haydn Jones's parliamentary career was to say the least uneventful. In his thirty-five years service he never made a speech on the floor of the House. *The Times* obituary notice described him as the ideal county member who served his Merioneth constituents with untiring devotion. He was not an eloquent speaker and had few popular gifts, but was strong willed, with great tenacity of purpose. He grew up in Towyn, where he joined his uncle's ironmongers business and eventually became the owner. He later became a member and alderman of Merioneth County Council and for some years was the honorary director of education for the County. He was survived by his wife and daughter.[44]

The scrap merchants removed all the quarry machinery including the internal tramway rails and the exit tramway as far as Alltwyllt Incline. A few small items were overlooked, such as bearing pedestals, parts of the Broad Vein water-

[44] *The Times,* 3 July 1950.

wheel and various objects underground. The reservoirs remained until fears for the safety of the dams led to their being drained and the dams breached. Certain chamber roofs were dynamited, leaving the gaping holes and broken rock marking the Narrow Vein today.

The survival of the quarry after 1910 in the face of increasing competition from manufactured roofing tiles and in spite of the best rock being already worked out was remarkable. It was essentially a job creation exercise and depended on the willingness of the men to accept low wages and working conditions which were primitive even by the standards of the slate industry. Many preferred to try their hand elsewhere, either going to other quarries or to the coal mines of South Wales, whilst others chose to emigrate.

The Gwernol Valley displays many of features which characterise Wales — mountain scenery, sheep farming, mineral exploitation, forestry and tourism. The industry which blossomed during the mining investment boom of the 1860s led to a large influx of population, dependent on the quarry for their livelihood. The railway was their lifeline, providing economic transport for the slate which they produced and a reliable delivery service for goods inward. The rise of trade unionism and the conflict between masters and men was followed by industrial decline, depopulation and a return to agriculture, though of a different kind. Sheep have always grazed the valley slopes but their domains are now threatened by the dark green monotony of the advancing conifer plantations. Today tourists come in their thousands to walk the trails where St. Cadvan reputedly trod thirteen centuries ago. The Gwernol Valley has truly been described as a microcosm of Wales.

2

Quarry Workings

COMMERCIALLY the most important slate beds, or veins, in the Corris District were the Vaen Gul (Narrow Vein) and the Vaen Galed (Hard or Broad Vein), and Bryneglwys had extensive workings in both. The ground lying between the rivers Dysynni and Dyfi consists mainly of beds of metamorphosed sedimentary rocks formed from fine particles of mud deposited beneath ancient seas some 450-600 million years ago, in the Upper Ordovician period, accumulating to great depths and consolidating under pressure into mudstones and shales. Later earth movements forced the rocks of North Wales upwards, leaving the strata of the Corris District dipping steeply to the south-east. The enormous lateral pressure which acted upon the rocks altered them into slate, the cleavage planes at Bryneglwys being almost vertical.

The course of the Narrow Vein from the coast at Tywyn to Dinas Mawddwy is marked by a series of quarries, some of them mere scratchings in the hillside and others extensively developed. First appearing near Esguan Hall above the Aberdyfi road (see fig. 1), it strikes along the south side of the Talyllyn Valley, through Dolgoch Ravine and Bryneglwys to Upper Corris. There it curves southwards to Braichgoch where it doubles sharply back on itself and resumes its north-easterly course to pass through Aberllefenni, Ratgoed and Hendre-ddu. The strike then becomes erratic and at Minllyn the vein disappears. The Narrow Vein is only 54 feet (16.5 m) thick and is composed of dark blue-grey, pure slate rock.[1 2 3]

[1] R. M. Jehu, 'The geology of the district around Towyn and Abergynolwyn', *Quarterly Journal of the Geological Society*, vol. 82, p. 65.
[2] W. J. Pugh, 'The geology of the district around Corris and Aberllefenni', *QJGS*, vol. 79, p. 508.
[3] W. J. Pugh, 'Geology of the district around Dinas Mawddwy', *QJGS*, vol. 84, p. 345.

SURFACE PLAN, BROAD VEIN

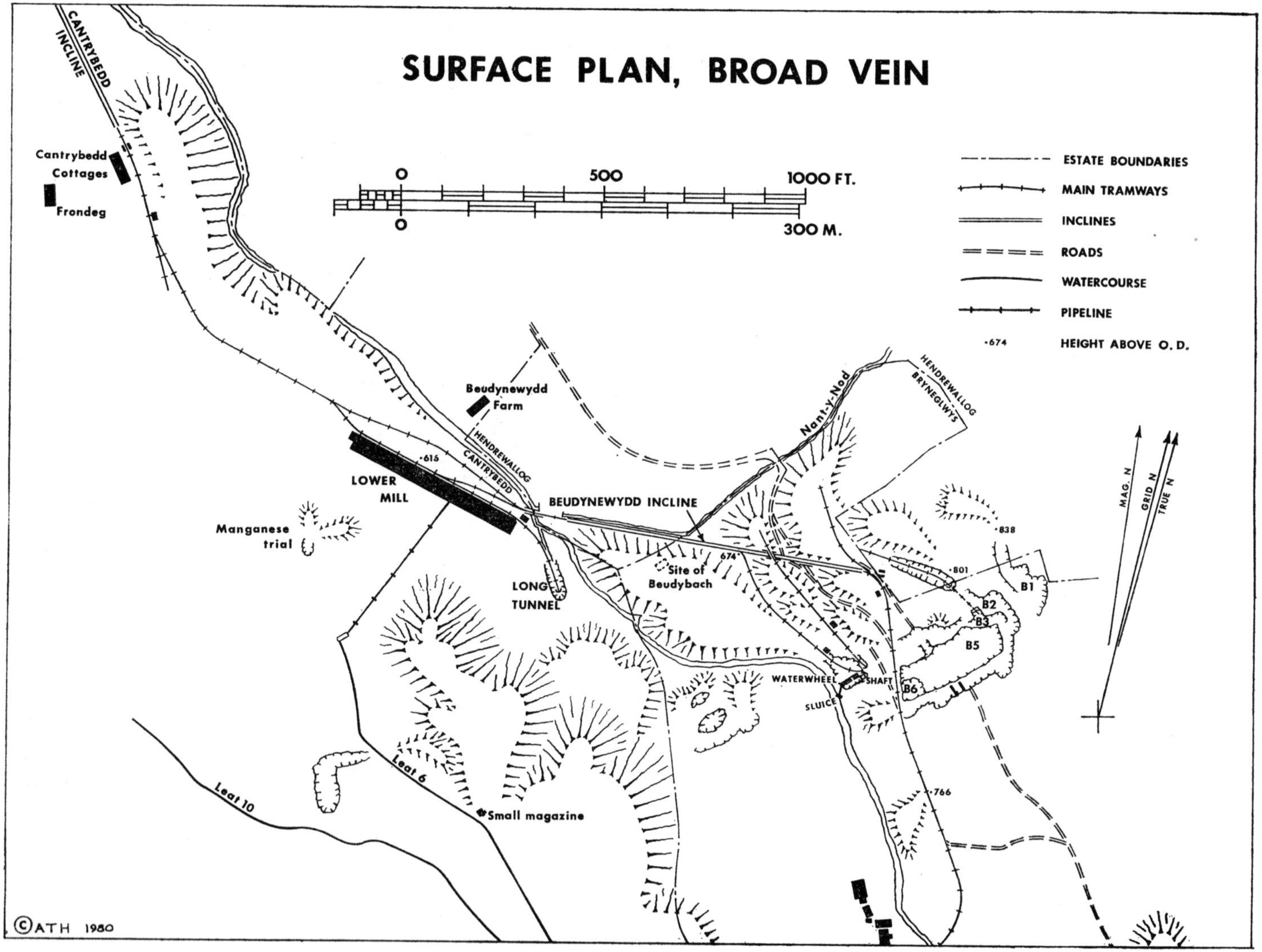

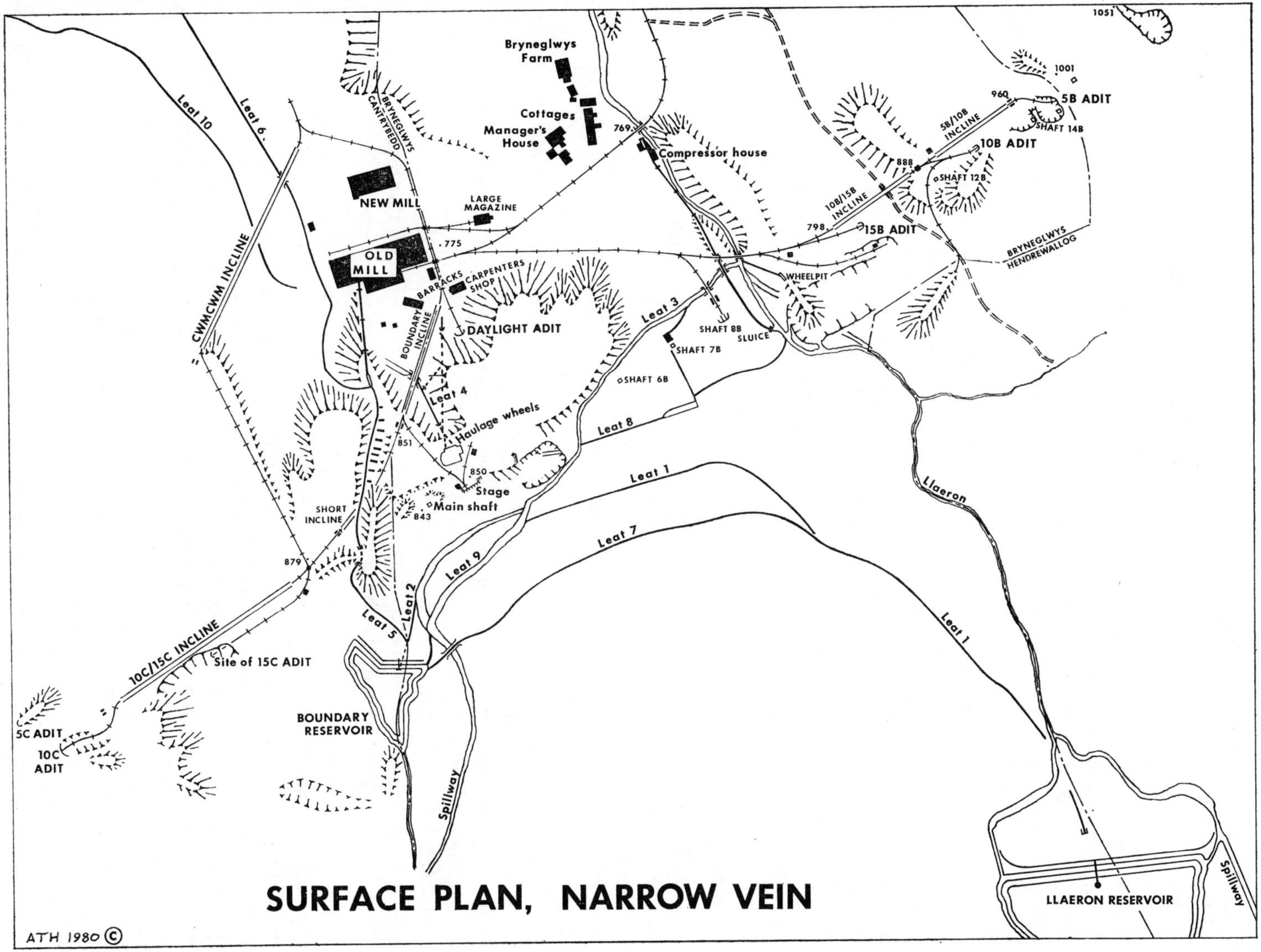

SURFACE PLAN, NARROW VEIN
ATH 1980 ©
Leat 10
Leat 6
BRYNEGLWYS CANTRYBEDD
Bryneglwys Farm
Cottages
Manager's House
769
Compressor house
NEW MILL
LARGE MAGAZINE
OLD MILL
775
BARRACKS
CARPENTERS SHOP
DAYLIGHT ADIT
BOUNDARY INCLINE
CWMCWM INCLINE
Leat 4
Haulage wheels
851
850
Stage
Main shaft
843
SHORT INCLINE
879
Leat 3
SHAFT 8B
SHAFT 7B
SLUICE
SHAFT 6B
Leat 8
Leat 1
Leat 7
Leat 9
Leat 2
Leat 5
10C/15C INCLINE
Site of 15C ADIT
5C ADIT
10C ADIT
BOUNDARY RESERVOIR
Spillway
1051
1001
960
5B ADIT
SHAFT 14B
5B/10B INCLINE
10B ADIT
888
SHAFT 12B
10B/15B INCLINE
798
15B ADIT
WHEELPIT
BRYNEGLWYS HENDREWALLOG
Llaeron
LLAERON RESERVOIR

Figure 3

Immediately below the Narrow Vein lies the Red Vein. It is about 350 feet (107 m) thick and although prospectors have tried it at several places, little commercial value was attached to it. Next comes the Broad Vein, second only to the Narrow Vein in importance, and some 1,500 feet (457 m) thick. It yielded slate of a pale blue-grey colour, but the quality varies considerably within the Vein. The Broad, Red and Narrow Vein sequence has no counterpart in the Ordovician rocks of Ffestiniog. South of Corris and also near Pennal there are several quarries known as 'Chwareli Damreiniol' (Accidental Quarries) located in slate rocks of the Silurian period.

The usual practice in the larger Narrow Vein quarries was to work the slate below ground in mines, although the term quarry was generally used when referring to undeground as well as surface workings. The actual methods used to win the slate differed from one quarry to another according to the dip of the strata and other factors, but they generally involved opening chambers within the vein. A chamber was formed by driving a tunnel into the slate rock and opening out a working space big enough to enable the rockmen to remove slabs of rock by drilling and blasting. As time went by and more slate was taken the chamber would extend across the full thickness of the vein and, at Bryneglwys, reached thirty yards (27 m) in length.

The dip of the Narrow Vein, that is the angle of slope of the bedding plane to the horizontal, varies. At Aberllefenni it is 70 degrees but at Bryneglwys it is shallower, varying between 50 and 60 degrees. The cleavage plane is nearly vertical and roughly parallel to the line of strike, the line across country where the vein appears at the surface. Along the cleavage planes the slate splits readily into thin sheets and this of course is the property that makes the rock commercially valuable. The cleavage plane must not be confused with the bedding plane, in fact they are inclined to one another at 30-40 degrees at Bryneglwys. There are other planes of weakness which help the rockman to cut blocks from the rockface. Vertical 'pillaring' occurs at right angles to the cleavage and usually leads to a wrinkled fracture surface along the edge of the block. 'Foot joints' appear sometimes and form horizontal planes of weakness.

To extract a block of slate the rockmen drill rows of holes in the face where the rock is to be cut, choosing the spot carefully in order to minimise the amount of blasting required. The aim is to produce blocks of roughly rectangular shape, weighing up to a ton. The traditional drilling tool is the jumper, a long steel rod sharpened to a cutting edge at the end. It was driven into the rock by hand, one man wielding a hammer and his partner holding the jumper, rotating it after each blow. In this way they would drill about 6 feet (1.8 m) depth in a day. Gunpowder was placed into the holes using a long handled copper scoop, and sealed with clay tamped in with a brass rod. Powder was preferred to high explosives because it caused less shattering of the rock, enabling large blocks to be extracted with the minimum of waste. The explosion caused a shock wave to travel through the rock, fracturing it hopefully along the intended planes. Large blocks arising from the blast would be split with chisels and wedges into pieces of a size convenient for loading onto trolleys and running out on tramways laid in the access tunnels.

The skilled men worked in teams and were paid on a contract system. Each team made a contract or 'bargain' with the Agent for the duration of a quarry month of four weeks. Other men — labourers, journeymen and assistants — were paid a fixed day wage. The system sometimes led to large differences in wages between skilled and unskilled contractors and day-men. Mr. Caradog Jones describes it:

> The only bad thing I felt there was that there was too much difference in wages between the contractors and the men who worked for day wages. There were two rockmen working in the chambers and two splitters in the mills. They worked as a team on contract, then there were journeymen working underground and a dresser in the mill. The contractors could earn very good money, up to £15 a month perhaps but the others were on 3/9d. (18½p) a day. For those that were working hard, they were earning very small money. You could be lucky the following Monday after the end of a month to have half a crown (12½p), just as a tip but not all would give you one. they kept everything for themselves. The system was very uneven, you could feel that amongst the workmen, especially the young people bringing up families, it was very hard on them.
>
> Even in my time I was receiving three pounds in a fortnight on one pay and five pounds at the end of the month, eight pounds total or two pounds per week. Now the man I was working with, he was receiving perhaps fifteen pounds — it depended on the contract you see. For every pound's worth of slate he got one pound bounty on top. The snag was that for every fifty slates you sold, you had to put sixty-six in to cover breakages.

Early workings

On the Narrow Vein, quarries were generally established at places where a stream intersected it, cutting a deep valley which allowed a series of levels to be formed, occasionally as open galleries but more often underground workings. This was the case at Bryneglwys, and although it isn't possible to say exactly where the first workings were, there are old levels which clearly predate those established in the major developments of the 1860s. On Cantrybedd there is an exposed rockface above the entrance to floor 10C which was worked as an open quarry (see figure 3). It was approached by a shallow cutting which now ends abruptly at the edge of the main cutting, some twelve feet (3.7 m) above the 10C level. A small hut stands alongside the waste tip, built of unmortared, unsawn pieces of slab. It is but four feet (1.2 m) high inside, has a narrow entrance and a small neatly built fireplace. Though there is trimming waste nearby (small flakes of rock formed when slates are trimmed to size) indicating that slates were made there, the hut is too dark inside to be a slatemakers hut (wal) and it may have been used as a barrack by one or two men.

On Bryneglwys there is an early cutting a few feet above floor 10B which must have been used before the adit was driven, the working again being an open face. The grass grown tip is still visible. The earliest developments which we can date were the work of John Pughe, who built a mill in 1847 close to the

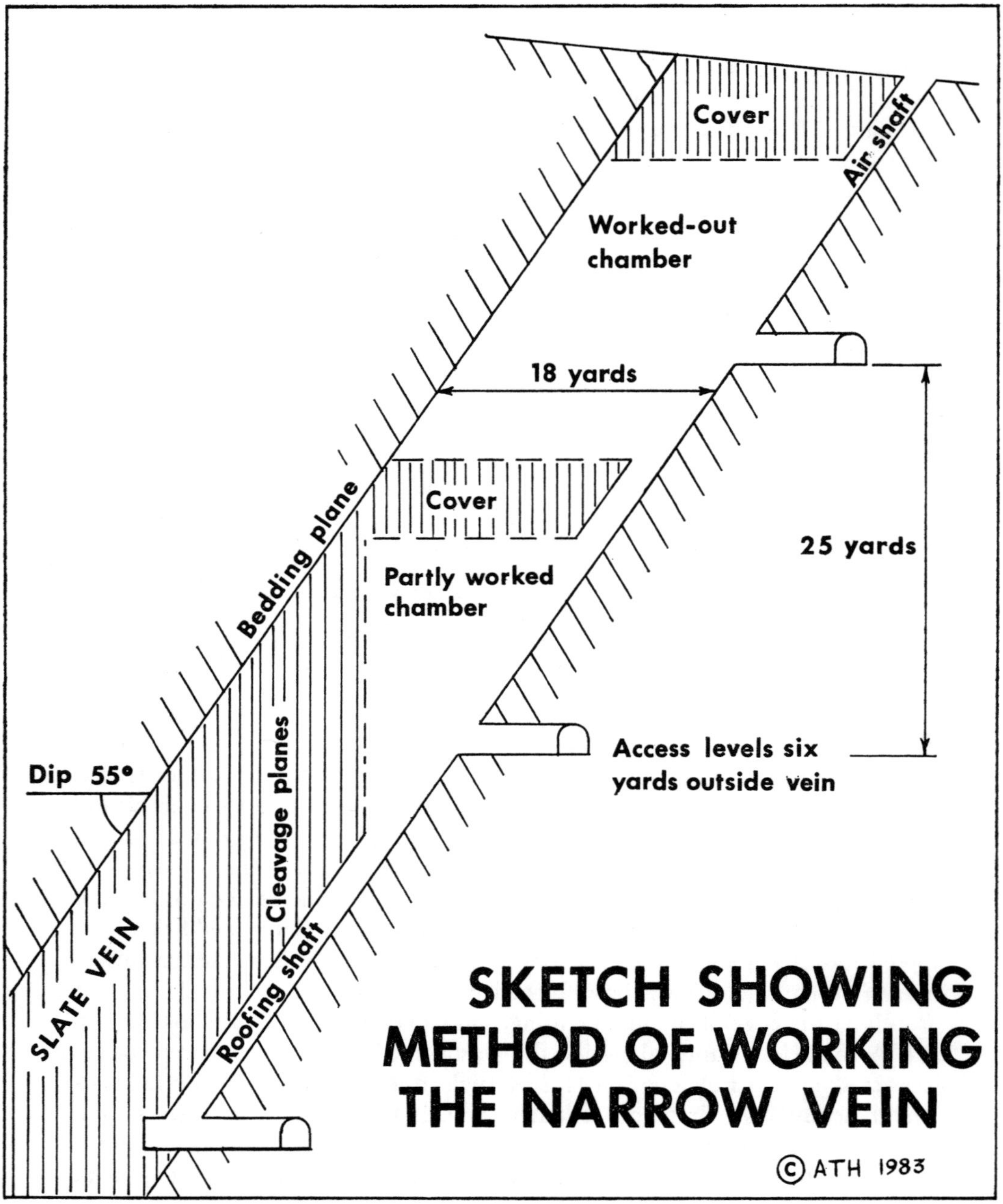
Cover
Air shaft
Worked-out chamber
18 yards
Cover
Bedding plane
Partly worked chamber
25 yards
Cleavage planes
Access levels six yards outside vein
Dip 55°
SLATE VEIN
Roofing shaft
SKETCH SHOWING METHOD OF WORKING THE NARROW VEIN
© ATH 1983

Figure 4

Boundary Stream and drove a tunnel known as the Daylight Adit from the mill towards the slate vein, where it ended in an open shaft. As the slate was worked away the shaft was gradually opened outwards to form a pit or twll. A manager's report of 1857 states that there were three such 'pits' being worked, probably on the sites of chambers 3B, 4B and 5B although 5B remained covered, only the air shaft reaching the surface.[4]

Pughe's quarry was compact and easy to work. The mill was reasonably close to the quarry face, there was ample room for tipping and there was no need for powered machinery such as lifting gear, pumps, etc., and the saws in the mill were hand operated. Although the quarry had considerable potential, development on a large scale required a major investment of capital to drive new levels, intall water power and above all a railwav to transport the produce to the port of Aberdyfi.

In 1862 Robert Williams extended the workings along the vein and also downwards below mill level. He opened two new faces, one on Cantrybedd and one on the Cantrybedd Bryneglwys boundary. The downward extension meant that mechanical power was needed to raise the slate blocks and rubbish and to drive the pump to drain the workings.[5]

Main development of the quarry

Following their purchase of the quarry, the Aberdovey Slate Company initiated major new developments along a different plan. The open pit method of working was not suited to the Narrow Vein at Bryneglwys since the angle of dip is only about 55 degrees and the overhang of the rock above the vein increased alarmingly as the workings went deeper. Instead of open pits the new plan was to mine the slate underground in chambers. The mine was developed on a series of floors at vertical intervals of 75 feet (23 m). On each floor a tunnel was driven parallel to the vein but outside it so as not to spoil good rock, and at regular intervals openings were cut from the tunnel into the vein. Chambers were started at each opening to provide working space for the slate blocks to be quarried. A 'roofing' shaft was first cut upwards by the miners above the opening, sometimes through to the chamber on the floor above or to the surface. This assisted ventilation and was used in some chambers to pass blocks up or down to a level having tramway access to the mills, (see figure 4).

The chamber was established by forming an enlarged space to provide a working face with two sides and a free top. The rockmen then took over and proceeded to cut rectangular blocks or slabs from the working face. This process continued until the chamber was worked out, which could take twenty years or so. The rock between the chambers was not cut, or was not supposed to be cut, and formed a wall some 30 feet (9 m) thick to support the roof, each wall being vertically in line with the ones on the floors above and below. A roof or 'cover' 15 feet (4.5 m) thick was left between successive floors, although many have been

[4] *NLW* Annual Report, 1973-4, p. 38, Deposit of Edward Davies Papers, Report by George Smith.
[5] NLW Ms. 8412.

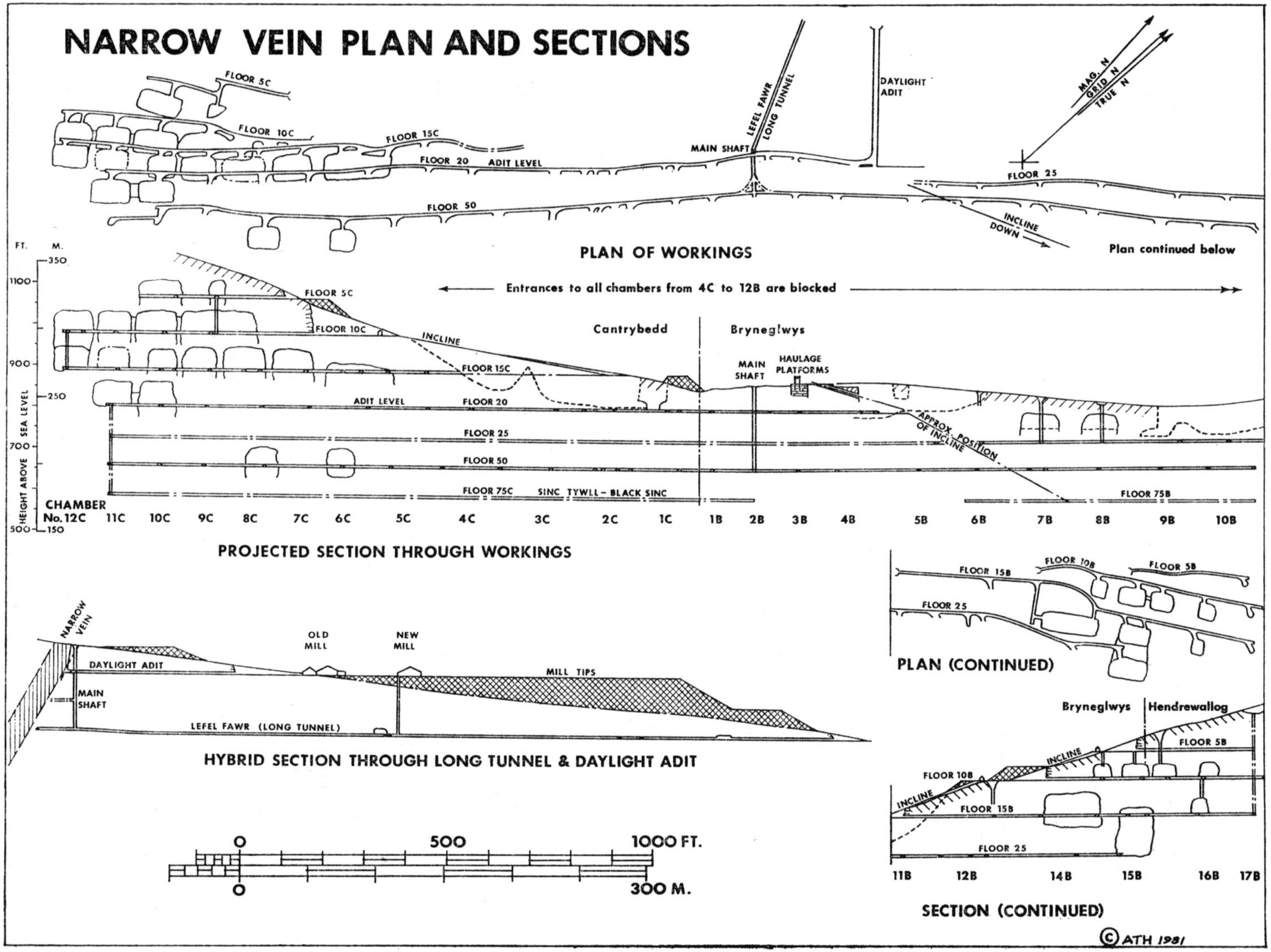
NARROW VEIN PLAN AND SECTIONS
FLOOR 5C
FLOOR 10C
FLOOR 15C
FLOOR 20
ADIT LEVEL
FLOOR 50
MAIN SHAFT
LEFEL FAWR
LONG TUNNEL
DAYLIGHT ADIT
MAG. N
GRID N
TRUE N
FLOOR 25
INCLINE DOWN
PLAN OF WORKINGS
Plan continued below
Entrances to all chambers from 4C to 12B are blocked
FT.
M.
350
1100
900
250
700
500
150
HEIGHT ABOVE SEA LEVEL
INCLINE
Cantrybedd
Bryneglwys
MAIN SHAFT
HAULAGE PLATFORMS
APPROX. POSITION OF INCLINE
FLOOR 75C
SINC TYWLL - BLACK SINC
FLOOR 75B
CHAMBER No. 12C
11C
10C
9C
8C
7C
6C
5C
4C
3C
2C
1C
1B
2B
3B
4B
5B
6B
7B
8B
9B
10B
PROJECTED SECTION THROUGH WORKINGS
FLOOR 15B
FLOOR 10B
FLOOR 5B
PLAN (CONTINUED)
NARROW VEIN
OLD MILL
NEW MILL
MILL TIPS
LEFEL FAWR (LONG TUNNEL)
HYBRID SECTION THROUGH LONG TUNNEL & DAYLIGHT ADIT
Hendrewallog
0
500
1000 FT.
300 M.
11B
12B
14B
15B
16B
17B
SECTION (CONTINUED)
© ATH 1981

Figure 5

partly or wholly worked away. In section the mine therefore appeared as a grid pattern of chambers 90 feet long, separated by walls and roofs of uncut rock. To extend the workings new floors could be driven deeper underground or existing ones extended along the vein.

Initially two levels were established at 75 and 150 feet (23 m and 46 m) below Adit level, as the mill level was called, and became floors 25 and 50 respectively. The Adit level was later designated floor 20. Further levels were driven above Adit level on each estate. There were three on Cantrybedd, 5C, 10C and 15C with the same nominal 75 feet (23 m) vertical interval between them. The Adit level was not extended on the Bryneglwys side as the depth below the surface was inadequate, but three new levels 5B, 10B and 15B were established with 15B lying 75 feet (23 m) above floor 25. Surface tramways connected all these workings to the Old Mill except for 5C which was purely a prospecting level before 1910.

The chambers were identified by numbers, each estate having its own series. Thus 4C for example was the fourth chamber on Cantrybedd counting from the boundary, and similarly for Bryneglwys using the letter B. The numbering did not distinguish between different floors. By 1879 there were eight chambers on Cantrybedd, the levels reaching a point 1,148 feet (348 m) from the boundary, whilst on Bryneglwys there were at that time sixteen chambers plus a surface working at 17B. A section through the vein showing the mine as it was when we surveyed it is shown on figure 5.

Adits and shafts

The key to these developments of the mine was the 'Lefel Fawr' or Long Tunnel and the Main Shaft which meets it. The tunnel is 1,935 feet long (589.9 m) and at its inner end meets floor 50. The entrance is approached from a cutting near the foot of Beudynewydd Incline, and it is dead straight as far as the Main Shaft, a distance of 1,844 feet (562.2m). It then veers to the left, meeting floor 50 at right angles to the vein, although there are two tramway tunnels branching off it to connect with each leg of that floor. The top of the Main Shaft lies on open ground opposite chamber 2B where there are some spoil heaps but no trace of any headframe or staging. It is 204 feet (62.2 m) deep and opens onto the Adit level tunnel (floor 20) and it is likely that as it was dug below that depth the spoil was brought out through floor 20. The tips at the surface evidently represent the arisings from the upper part of the shaft, above Adit level. A second shaft was dug close to the bank of the Boundary Stream, which had by then been diverted, on the site of the ancient stone circle 785 feet (239.3 m) from the Main Shaft. As the stream bed was filled in and the ground levelled by tipping rubbish, a slab retaining wall was built up around the mouth of the shaft so that the present surface lies 25 feet (7.62 m) above the original level. The New Mill was built on this ground, the shaft actually lying within the floor plan of the building. The two shafts gave four extra working faces for driving the Long Tunnel, which probably took about two years to finish.

There is another shaft near the Long Tunnel, shown as an air shaft on the

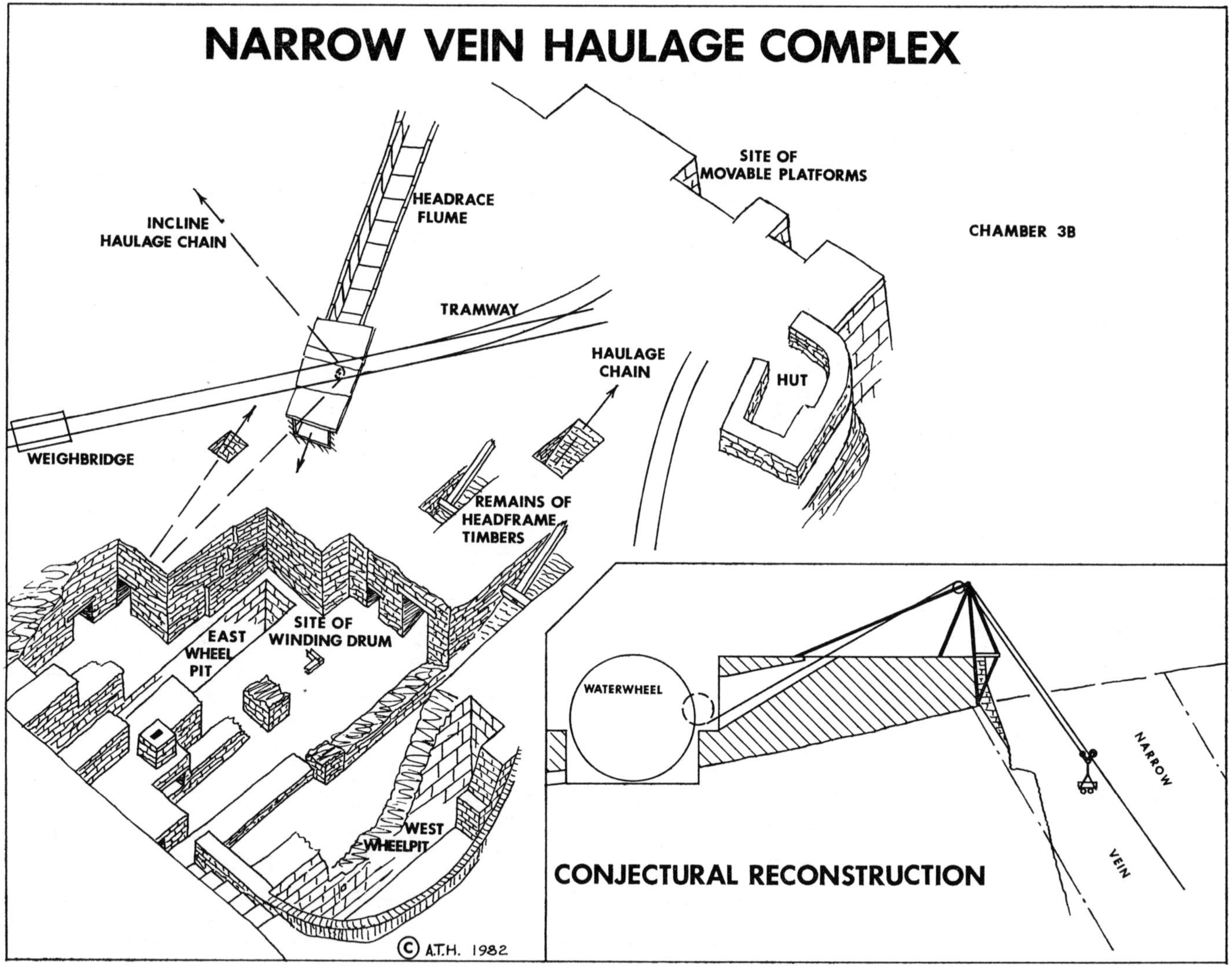
NARROW VEIN HAULAGE COMPLEX
SITE OF MOVABLE PLATFORMS
CHAMBER 3B
INCLINE HAULAGE CHAIN
HEADRACE FLUME
TRAMWAY
HAULAGE CHAIN
HUT
WEIGHBRIDGE
REMAINS OF HEADFRAME TIMBERS
EAST WHEEL PIT
SITE OF WINDING DRUM
WEST WHEELPIT
© A.T.H. 1982
WATERWHEEL
NARROW
VEIN
CONJECTURAL RECONSTRUCTION

Figure 6

first edition Ordnance Survey plans (surveyed in 1887) and later filled in with rubbish. It may have been used in driving the Long Tunnel, to which it is connected by a branch 35 feet (10.7 m) long.

Completion of the Long Tunnel meant that the mine was dry down to floor 50, which connected directly with it. Floor 25 also connected with the Main Shaft for drainage and both were served by the haulage system for raising blocks and rubbish (waste rock) though rubbish from 50 was probably also taken out through the Long Tunnel.

Later a new floor 75 was opened below 50 in two unconnected sections. Because they lay below the Long Tunnel pumps had to be installed to keep the workings dry, one in each section, but it is unclear why the two workings were not joined and served by common hoist and pump systems. Floor 75 became the notorious 'Black Sinc' (Sinc Dywyll), an appelation which came to symbolise what was a very damp, dirty and dangerous place.

As the chambers were worked out the floors were extended westwards on Cantrybedd. By the 1900s there were twelve chambers but by then the dangerous and all too common practice of working away the walls and roofs had started. This was a cheaper way to win slate than opening a new chamber, and by 1910 for instance chambers 3C and 6C on floors 25 and 50 had become one vast chamber. Waste rock was tipped into the worked out chambers and this helped to support the rock and prevent the sides from falling in. The surface tramway inclines from the higher levels fell into disuse, the slate blocks being lowered underground instead. This was done using two-handled winches, allowing the blocks to slide down the face of the rocks on a chain. The winch consisted of a stout cast iron frame supporting the winding drum for the chain and two gear trains; one a double reduction giving a ratio of 13.4 to 1, the other a single reduction of 6.9 to 1. Pawl and ratchet mechanisms helped to prevent runaways but accidents did occur and the rapidly rotating handles took their toll of broken jawbones and other injuries. In use, the winch was set on the floor of the access tunnel to the chamber and chocked securely against the roof with a baulk of timber. A pulley was mounted on the top edge of the rockface to guide the chain and prevent it chafing against the rock. By this means blocks were lowered for example from floor 5C to 10C and from there to 15C where they could be taken out to the Old Mill via the Cwmcwm Incline. Several winches remain *in situ,* notably in floors 15C and 25.

Haulage systems

Robert Williams erected a surface landing stage with an inclined chain hoist system similar to those used in his native Nantlle district quarries such as Dorothea,[6] probably in 1862-3. A sketch of the remains and a tentative reconstruction are shown on figure 6. To support the landing platform and headframe he built a massive slab footwall which still exists on the north side of the opening

[6] D. C. Davies, 'Slate and Slate Quarrying', 5th edition, Crosby Lockwood and Son, (1912), fig. 32.

above chamber 3B. The main chain ran from the top of the headframe down through the open chamber to a level roughly corresponding to floor 25, where it was anchored to solid rock. A pulley block travelled along it and supported a main suspension chain and four short chains which were hooked to the corners of the wagon being raised or lowered. A traction chain or cable drew the block, carrying its load, up to the landing. This consisted of a movable platform, essentially a flap which was raised on hinges out of the way as the load came up, the lowered to take the weight of the wagon so that the chains could be released and the wagon run off to the tramway. The headframe was braced by massive timber struts supported by masonary some 50 feet (15 m) back from the landing. The ends of two struts survive. One is 9 ins. × 8 ins. (229 mm × 203 mm) in cross section and it is tenoned into a stout cross piece bedded into masonry at each end. There were apparently two haulage chains and platforms, the whole thing being typical of the individual, locally made structures built to meet the quarry's own particular needs.

Rubbish raised by the hoist was tipped on the ground conveniently close to the landing, forming the large fan of tips above the Daylight Adit, and a tramway transported the blocks to the mill via the Boundary Incline, which lay on the border between Bryneglwys and Cantrybedd. A water wheel 30 feet (9.1 m) in diameter and 3 feet (.92 m) wide provided power for the hoists and for the pump used to drain the workings before the Long Tunnel was completed. Later another similar wheel was added and the winding machinery installed in he space between them. The wheels and machinery were removed, probably in 1910, but the wheelpit, tailrace culverts and stonework remain. The wheelpits are of massive blocks of dressed slabs and originally stood up above ground level, but as the arisings of rubbish from the mine were tipped all around them they became buried. Eventually a slab retaining wall had to be erected around the site so that the final surface of the rubbish lies 30 feet (9.15 m) above the base of the wheelpits. The haulage chains ran through special openings in the retaining wall to the headframe. A roofed cabin was provided for the operators and a flight of steps leads down to it from the surface. Another stairway was built on the opposite side of the site and was totally enclosed within the stonework. It was blanked off by a later haulage chain tunnel, probably when the second wheel was installed. A slab at the entrance bears the graffito 'John Whiting 1866'.

The next development of the haulage system was an incline laid within the vein, its summit being level with and connected by tramway to the Daylight Adit and running down towards the north-east, probably to floor 50. One of the waterwheels drove the winding gear for working the incline. The haulage chain ran through the tunnel which was built up of slabs, and turned a corner to bring it into line with the incline. Inside the tunnel there are pulleys of various sizes used to guide the chain, which emerged through an opening in a wall above chamber 4B. The opening is 39 feet (11.9 m) above Adit Level, the distance in a direct line to the top of the incline being about 130 feet (39.6 m). Nothing is visible of the incline itself owing to the collapse of the chambers which it passed

A recent view of the access tunnel on Floor 10c. The roof clearly shows the angle of dip of the bedding planes, and several chamber entrances are visible on the left.

(R. Thomas)

Inside chamber No. 10 on Floor 5C, looking south-east with the slate vein dipping downwards to the right. The chamber entrance is about halfway down the left hand side of the photograph.

(R. Thomas)

Inside 15C adit. A rubbish wagon stands on the tramway and a branch leads into a chamber on the left. A winch lies near the wagon, and another at the next chamber entrance tunnel.

(R. Thomas)

Another view of the rubbish wagon in the previous picture.

(Author)

Close-up of the winch in the same picture.

(Author)

A trolley loaded with a large slab en route to the mills, probably at the entrance to 15C adit.

(Caradog Jones collection)

Mr. Caradog Jones in the Village Museum and some of the tools in his collection. Slates were split with the hammer and chisel, lower right; the edges were trimmed using the long knife, supporting the slate on the carrier or trafal (upper right). Lower left, a powder scoop and tamper used in laying the charge for blasting the rock.

(Author)

An early group posed in front of the Barracks, centre, and the Smithy on the right. It is said that the two bowler-hatted figures on the extreme right are the McConnels, father and son.

(Caradog Jones collection)

General view of the Upper Level buildings. The Manager's house is on the extreme left, the Old Mill is the large building in the right foreground and the Barracks is on the extreme right.

(Caradog Jones collection. Burrell's)

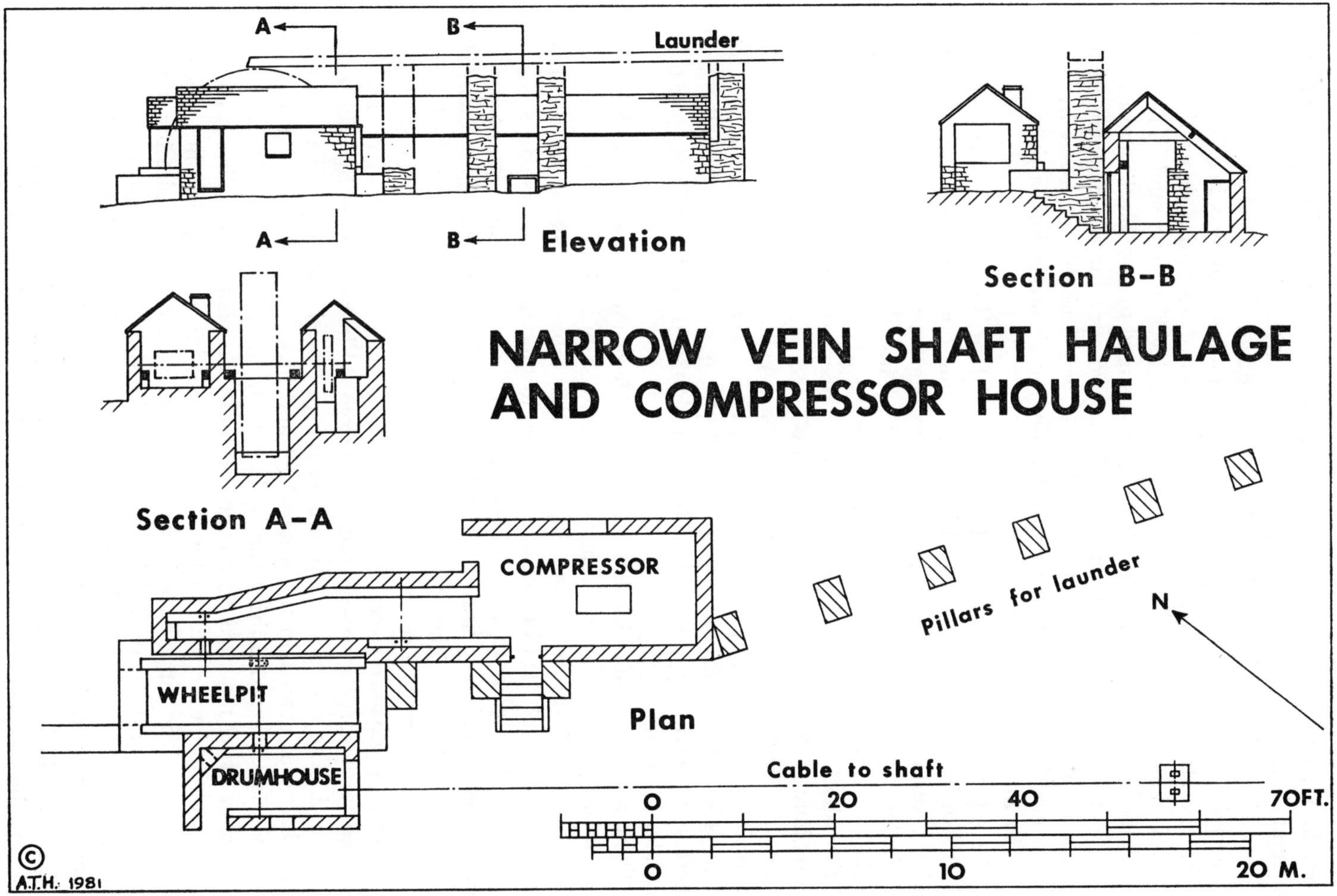
A
B
Launder
A
B
Elevation
Section B–B
NARROW VEIN SHAFT HAULAGE
AND COMPRESSOR HOUSE
Section A–A
COMPRESSOR
WHEELPIT
DRUMHOUSE
Plan
Pillars for launder
N
Cable to shaft
0
20
40
70FT.
0
10
20 M.
© A.T.H. 1981

Figure 7

through. Wagons from the incline were run on to a tramway leading into the Daylight Adit.

There is an inclined shaft from the surface down through chamber 7B and a wheelpit and plinth alongside suggest that winding gear was installed in the shaft. The absence of a tramway connection and of waste tips shows that stuff was raised not to the surface, but to another level underground. The likely explanation seems to be that the lifting gear was used to raise blocks and rubbish from floor 75 to floor 50. It cannot be followed very far down owing to the accumulation of rubbish in the chamber. It was probably removed by 1911 since a new hoist was installed under Haydn Jones's ownership in the adjacent chamber 8B.

The 8B system also consisted of an inclined shaft, but this time a track was laid down it so that wagons could be run up and down between the chambers and the surface. Inclined at an angle of 55 degrees it was by far the steepest rail incline at Bryneglwys. A new waterwheel installed alongside the Llaeron by the exit tramway bridge provided the motive power for the incline. All trace of the wheel has gone, but the pit is well preserved and shows that a wheel approximately 20 feet (6.1 m) diameter by 4 feet (1.2 m) breast was used, see figure 7. A hut, or drumhouse, containing a fireplace on the west side of the wheelpit had an opening in one end wall facing the 8B shaft some 450 feet away. The haulage cables passed through the opening and crossed the field where they were supported by pulleys on slab and timber pillars spaced at irregular intervals.

There are two substantial slab walls either side of the tramway just above the shaft mouth, similar to a conventional drumhouse but without a roof. Wooden beams straddled the walls and supported the cables by means of overhung pulleys. Because of the distance between the drumhouse and the shaft, a signalling system was used to tell the brakeman when to start and stop winding. Markers on the cables indicated when the 'run' had reached the top of the shaft.

As well as haulage, the wheel drove an air compressor to supply the rock drills, piping being laid in to 15B adit for example where it still survives. This was the only advance over hand drilling used on the Narrow Vein and was confined to the Bryneglwys chambers, Cantrybedd being worked by hand drills to the end. The compressor house is to the east of the wheelpit. The primary drive shaft was geared to the waterwheel and its outer end projected into the house where the onward drive was by belt, with an intermediate idler shaft, the compressor being mounted on a concrete plinth. In plan the building is narrow at one end, just wide enough for the drive belt, but it opens out in the compressor room. The pitched roof consequently has a curious but pleasing outline on the east side, the eaves height changing with the increase in span across the walls. A flight of steps leads down to the entrance on the west side and above the entrance a piece of inverted bridge rail serves as a makeshift gutter.

On Cantrybedd there was a waterwheel to drive a drainage pump on floor 75 and it probably also powered a hoist from there up to floor 50. According to a report written in 1910 it was located in a shaft at chamber 1C, but the collapse of the quarry at that point has obliterated the site and there are no visible remains.

Broad Vein workings

The Broad Vein was not worked as extensively as the Narrow Vein, or as systematically. We cannot date the earliest workings but it is likely that three main sites were being worked by 1881. Open levels were established above and below the road on Bryneglwys land above the top of Beudynewydd Incline. The road lay higher up the hillside than its present course, but it was diverted in 1882 to allow room for expansion of the working levels. The galleries were established at vertical intervals of 40 feet (12.2 m) and we have invented a designation for these levels in default of any known official one. The highest was B1 at 838 feet (255.5 m) but it remained undeveloped, merely a trial working. Next came B2, but little of it remains now because of the advance of B3. B3 was on the same level as the exit tramway (762 feet, 232.3m) and B4 was approached by a tunnel below the tramway. Lower still was B5, reached by an adit driven along the vein, with a tramway connection to a point part way up Beudynewydd Incline. A section through the Broad Vein appears on figure 8.

Space for tipping was a problem on the Broad Vein, just as it was on the Narrow. The Llaeron was diverted to allow further tipping from B5 but only at the expense of levelling some old tips on the other side of the river. It is unclear why a culvert was not provided, possibly there was a fear that it would be inadequate to cope with the river in full spate. Access for tipping from B3 was improved by driving a tunnel, approached by a long cutting, behind Beudynewydd drumhouse. This replaced the awkward arrangement which used the exit tramway, with a branch crossing the incline tracks just in front of the drumhouse. Tipping from B4 was extended bv a tramway laid across the incline on a bridge whose abutments are built of enormous slabs.

Further development took place under Haydn Jones. A new floor B6, drained by a pump, was established by driving downwards from B5. As ever, tipping space was short, so the whole area between Beudynewydd Incline and the river was taken for tipping. Beudybach Cottage had to be abandoned and it now lies buried beneath 30 feet (9 m) of tipped rock. Even so, a raised ramp for waste tipping had to be built on B5, approached by a gradient from the working level. The road was diverted yet again, crossing the incline at track level in place of the underbridge of 1882, freeing some precious space for the B3 tips to be extended.

Water power was used to drive a compressor for the rockdrills and the pump for draining B6. An overshot wheel 18 feet (5.5 m) diameter by 4 feet (1.2 m) breast supplied by Williams and White of Aberystwyth, shown on figure 9, was installed just outside B5 Adit entrance. It had cast iron hubs carried on a massive forged axle, wooden spokes and cast iron rims. The sixty-four buckets were of tarred wooden boards which fitted into slots cast in the rims. An internally geared ring fixed to the spokes drove a pinion on an intermediate shaft which in turn drove a second intermediate shaft by belt and pulleys. The final drive

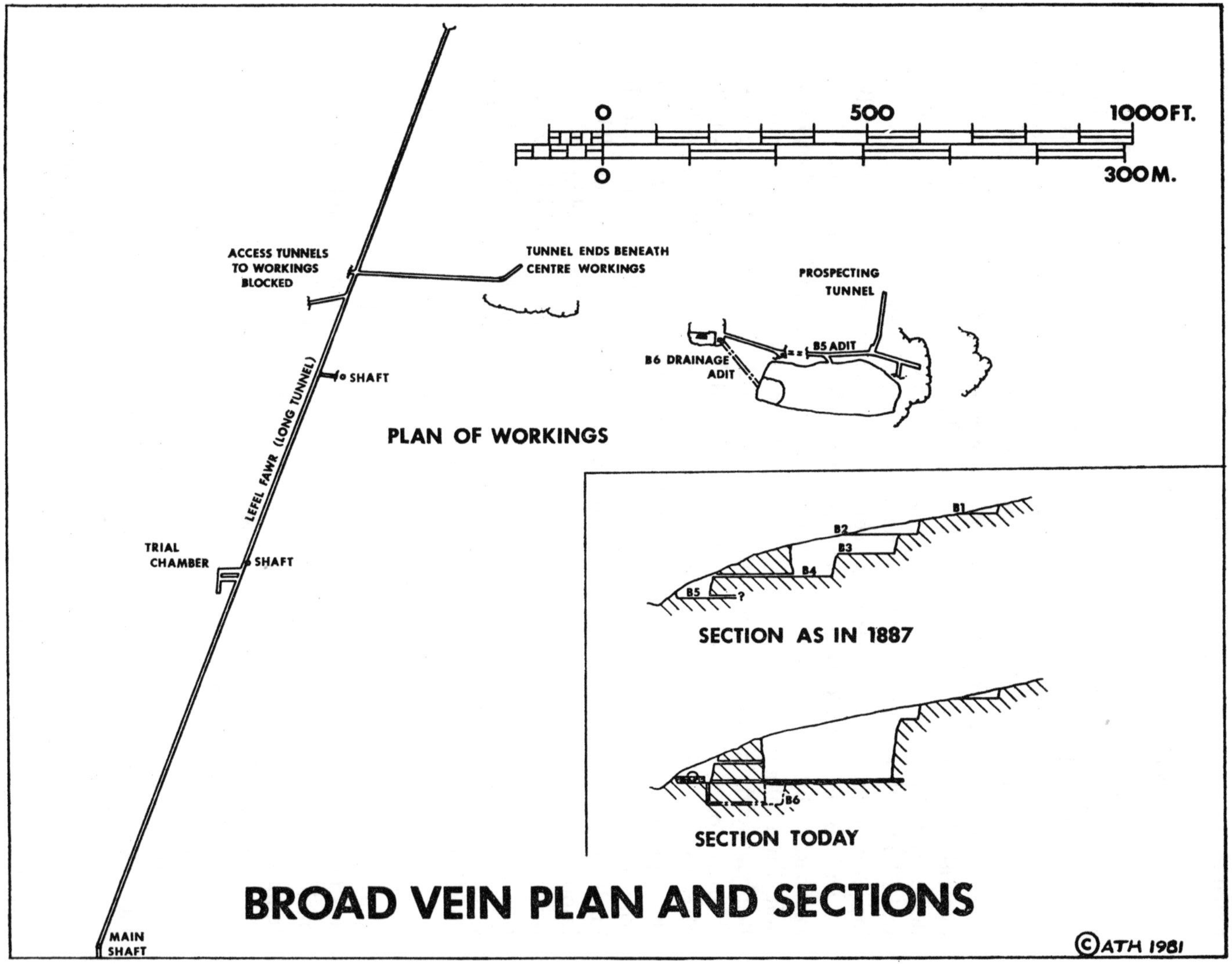
0
500
1000FT.
0
300M.
ACCESS TUNNELS TO WORKINGS BLOCKED
TUNNEL ENDS BENEATH CENTRE WORKINGS
PROSPECTING TUNNEL
B5 ADIT
B6 DRAINAGE ADIT
SHAFT
LEFEL FAWR (LONG TUNNEL)
PLAN OF WORKINGS
TRIAL CHAMBER
SHAFT
B1
B2
B3
B4
B5
?
SECTION AS IN 1887
B6
SECTION TODAY
BROAD VEIN PLAN AND SECTIONS
MAIN SHAFT
©ATH 1981

Figure 8

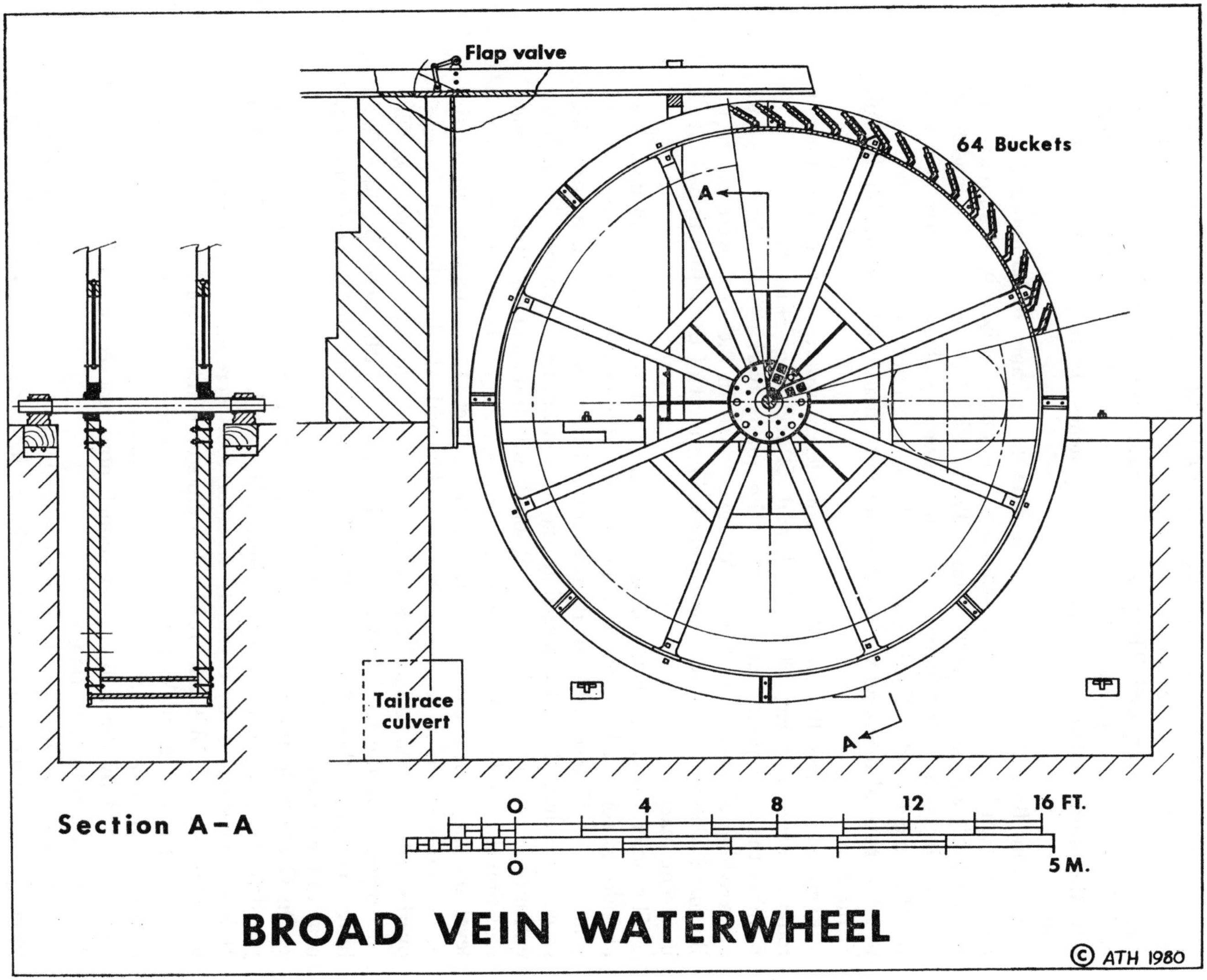
Flap valve
64 Buckets
A
A
Tailrace culvert
Section A–A
0
4
8
12
16 FT.
0
5 M.
BROAD VEIN WATERWHEEL
© ATH 1980

Figure 9

to the compressor was also by belt, the shaft centres being no less than 33 feet (10 m) apart. The intermediate shafts enabled the speed of the wheel to be matched to that of the compressor, a step up from 5 or 6 r.p.m. to about 250 r.p.m. being required. The primary gear ratio was approximately 4 to 1 and each intermediate drive was about 3½ to 1. The compressor has been removed, only the plinth remaining, but air piping 2½ inches (63 mm) bore remains in the adit.

To drain B6 a shaft was dug just outside the entrance to B5 and a drainage adit cut from its base to the B6 workings. The pump, driven by compressed air, was a double acting type by the Hardy Patent Pick Co., purchased second hand from Braichgoch Slate Quarry. The compressor was obtained nearly new from the Brittania Foundry, Porthmadog. A scheme to connect B6 to the Long Tunnel to allow natural drainage was mooted but not carried out, presumably because of the cost.

Eventually levels B4 and B5 were completely worked out so that there is today a hole 80 feet deep, 80 feet wide and 250 feet long (24 m × 24 m × 76 m) forming the most prominent feature of the quarry workings seen by the visitor approaching along the road from Abergynolwyn. In the south-west corner the B6 sinc is flooded, the water mercifully hiding most of the refuse tipped into it in recent years.

The other workings on the Broad Vein are far less obtrusive and have been abandoned for much longer. On the opposite side of the stream there are two shafts about 35 feet (10.8 m) deep connected at their base by a tunnel which extends northwards and emerged to daylight near the riverbank although the entrance is now blocked by a fall. Rubbish was trammed out from the tunnel and tipped near Beudybach Cottage. At the surface of the shafts the ground is level and has been cut back to a face some 15 feet (4.6 m) high, whilst the tips are so grass-grown as to merge imperceptibly with the hillside and are easily overlooked. Both shafts have been widened towards the top and a trial working was opened off the level between the shafts. Very little useful produce could have come from these desultory efforts. A branch from the Long Tunnel ends near to these workings but is not connected to them.

On Cantrybedd there is a fairly large fan of tips on the same level as those just described, but their source lies buried beneath later tips from the Old Mill. It is not possible to say definitely whether they were surface or underground workings, and the 1879 and 1881 sale catalogue plans do not help because they show none of the Broad Vein sites although they are referred to in general terms in the descriptions 7 and 8. The 1887 Ordnance Survey plan shows the site already buried by the mill tips. A tunnel, now blocked, leads from the Long Tunnel towards these workings.

There was one further attempt to exploit the Broad Vein, this time more recently. On Cantrybedd there is a cutting which ends in an open rockface which

[7] NLW 1879 Sale Catalogues (Merioneth), No. 3.
[8] NLW 1881 Sale Catalogues (Merioneth), No. 166.

is little more than a proving trial. The tip runs across the Mill tips at a higher level than the hidden workings described above.

The question of transport from the Broad Vein quarry faces to the mills before the opening of the Lower Mill in 1881 is problematical. According to the 1879 sale catalogue there was a steam crane and steam winches on the Vein. The O.S. plan shows a small building with a tramway passing through it near the Old Mill which must have been a drumhouse at the top of an incline leading to the Broad Vein workings. Since the blocks had to be hauled up the incline, power was needed and could have consisted of a steam-driven winch. There was a steam drill also mentioned in the catalogue, which would have provided additional load for the boiler, helping to justify its cost.

Floor B2 lay some 40 feet (12 m) above the tramway, and little produce came from it, but B4 was more productive and needed machinery to lift the blocks up to the tramway. A steam winch or crane was probably used for this purpose, and there are signs of an overhead ropeway across the B4/B5 working which raised wagons to B3 and the tramway. The site is marked by two slab walls on the south side of the pit and a gap in the rockwall on the opposite side. The tramway ran from this gap to join the exit tramway a short distance from Beudynewydd drumhouse. A tramway connection to Beudynewydd Incline from B5 enabled blocks to be taken direct to the Lower Mill from the time of its opening in 1881, and it seems likely that blocks from B6 were raised up to B5 and taken out the same way.

The quarry today

As the quarry is constantly deteriorating, this description applies to the survey period only (late 1970s) as new falls of rock cause more chambers to collapse or cut off whole sections of the underground workings.

On the Narrow Vein, floors 5B, 10B and 15B are accessible from their entrances, if somewhat precariously. At 59 feet (18 m) from the entrance, 5B adit is intersected by a shaft running from the surface down to chamber 15B in the floor below. At its innermost end it meets another shaft, now filled with rubbish, connected to the surface working 17B. Presumably, blocks from 17B were let down this shaft and taken out either via 5B or 10B. There are no chambers opened on floor 5B.

Floor 10B is flooded knee-deep at the entrance and extends as far as the shaft at 17B. There are four chambers on this floor, all still accessible. Chamber 14B has been opened from the outside and apparently worked from an intermediate level some 33 feet (10 m) above 10B adit. Why this was done is not clear, but it may have been to enable rubbish to be tipped much nearer to the chamber.

The next chamber, 15B, is in fact two chambers linked by an opening through the dividing wall. They are the largest chambers on this floor, and the roofing shaft which cuts through 5B adit rises above a gruesome pile of bones, the remains of sheep and cattle which have strayed into the shaft. Chamber 16B is small and has a shaft in the floor down to the chamber below. Some rails remain in the adit, stacked apparently awaiting removal, and sleepers of logs sawn lengthways in half were also found here.

The 10B waste tips lie on each side of the entrance on Bryneglwys land. Some of the chambers however are beneath Hendrewallog, and when Lewis Morris complained that the Company were tipping rubbish from 'other quarries' on his land in 1875, a new tramway was laid, crossing the road on the level, to take the wagons to a site beyond the boundary wall.

The entrance to 15B adit has collapsed, and the fallen portion of the roof contains timbers which were evidently put up to prevent the sides of the approach cutting from falling in. Track is still *in situ* for a distance of 505 feet (154 m) and is flooded with stagnant water to a depth of 14 inches (355 mm) at the entrance. At a point 480 feet (146 m) from the entrance the rails are at water level, giving an average gradient of 1 in 440.

A 3 inch (75 mm) diameter pipe is laid on brackets fixed to the south wall of the adit. Its purpose was to feed compressed air to the rock drills in the chambers. The entrance to the first chamber, 12B, is blocked but there is a shaft running into it from the surface near the 10B/15B drumhouse.

Beyond 12B there is a fault in the vein, and the adit turns through a dogleg before continuing on a straight course as far as the shaft up to 17B. A large chamber, 14B (there is no 13B) lies opposite the dogleg and has two entrances, the first being via a trial adit 99 feet (30 m) long at right angles to the main adit.

The next chamber, 15B, has a low roof but is opened right down to floor 25 below. It has two entrances, one carrying a $1\frac{1}{4}$ inch (32 mm) diameter air pipe teed off the 3 inch main. There is one other chamber, 16B, small and undeveloped, a roofing shaft connecting it with the floor above.

From chamber 15B it is an easy climb down to floor 25B which has no direct opening to the surface. From the access chamber it runs south-west for 1,412 feet (430 m) where it is blocked by a roof fall. There are ten chamber entrances along this portion of the adit, all blocked, leading to chambers 5B to 14B. Since there is no 13B, there must be one chamber with two entrances, probably 12B. Track remains *in situ* over most of the adit and there is also a winch. Beyond the roof fall, the floor is accessible from the main shaft and agile potholers report that it contains wagons still loaded with slate, tools, etc., evidently cut off after a working shift.

On the surface, the roofs of chambers 9B to 11B have collapsed and fresh rockfalls occur in this area from time to time. Chambers 7B and 8B are accessible from surface shafts but partly filled with waste rock. Chambers 1B to 6B have all collapsed at the surface.

The Daylight Adit is intact. The Adit Level is passable although dangerous in places, particularly by Chamber 1B where the roof has been shored with rails which have been bent or have fallen under stress. The adit is 12 feet (3.7 m) wide as far as the Main Shaft. Only the furthest chamber, 11C, is open to the adit although 10C can be entered from it by climbing up a series of iron pegs driven into the dividing wall. The floor of 10C is covered with rubble running down towards the back of the chamber.

Adits 10C and 5C are accessible, as are the chambers on these floors. A roofing shaft in chamber 9C connects the two levels, allowing blocks from 5C, which was not rail connected, to be lowered for dispatch to the mills. Chambers 8C and 9C are run together on floor 10C. There is a curious inclined tunnel near the entrance of 10C adit containing a capped shaft mouth leading down to chamber 7C on the floor below.

From chamber 12C it is possible to climb down to floor 15C. There are eight chambers, 5C to 12C, on this floor and all except 11C are accessible. There is some track, including turnouts, in the adit and also a rubbish wagon and several winches.

The Long Tunnel provides access to floor 50, though it is up to waist deep in running water. On Cantrybedd there were nine chambers on floor 50, but only two are accessible, and both are relatively small. The adit continues further to chambers 10C and 11C, but only the roofing shafts have been cut. The length of the adit up to its junction with the Long Tunnel is 1,584 feet (484 m) and the dip of the vein at this level is 58 degrees. The junction is opposite chamber 2B, now blocked, as are all eleven chambers on the Bryneglwys section of floor 50.

Floor 75 is completely inaccessible and is filled with water and rubble.

On the surface the original ground remains over the wall between chambers 1C and 2C but a gaping hole extends from there to the far end of chamber 5C, the Boundary Stream falling into the opening in the region of 2C. The entrance to 15C adit from the surface has collapsed.

The Broad Vein workings remain much as they were when the quarry closed, the principal feature being the large open pit by the road. B5 adit is blocked some 120 feet (36.6 m) from the entrance, but it can be entered from the far end via an opening in the pit. Two other adits, both short, survive on B3 and B4. From the Long Tunnel there are adits into the Broad Vein, but they are blocked and any chambers which may exist are inaccessible.

Most of the surface buildings on the Cantrybedd and Bryneglwys quarry estates have been demolished since our survey was completed. The tips will endure but even they are becoming clothed, like the hillsides around and above them, in the monotonous green of the forest plantations.

Annual output and employment figures

The official returns of annual slate tonnage produced are available for 1877-1909 and 1912-13.[9] For other years we have estimated the approximate output from the Talyllyn Railway annual returns, though these do not, unfortunately, distinguish between slate and other merchandise.[10] Some manuscript accounts for 1924-38 give the revenue from slates sold, and the output can be estimated roughly from these figures.[11] Employment statistics are known for 1877-87,

[9] Parliamentary Papers, Reports of the Mines Inspectorate.
[10] Parliamentary Papers, Annual Reports of the Board of Trade and Ministry of Transport.
[11] NLW Lady Haydn Jones deposits, Box 4.

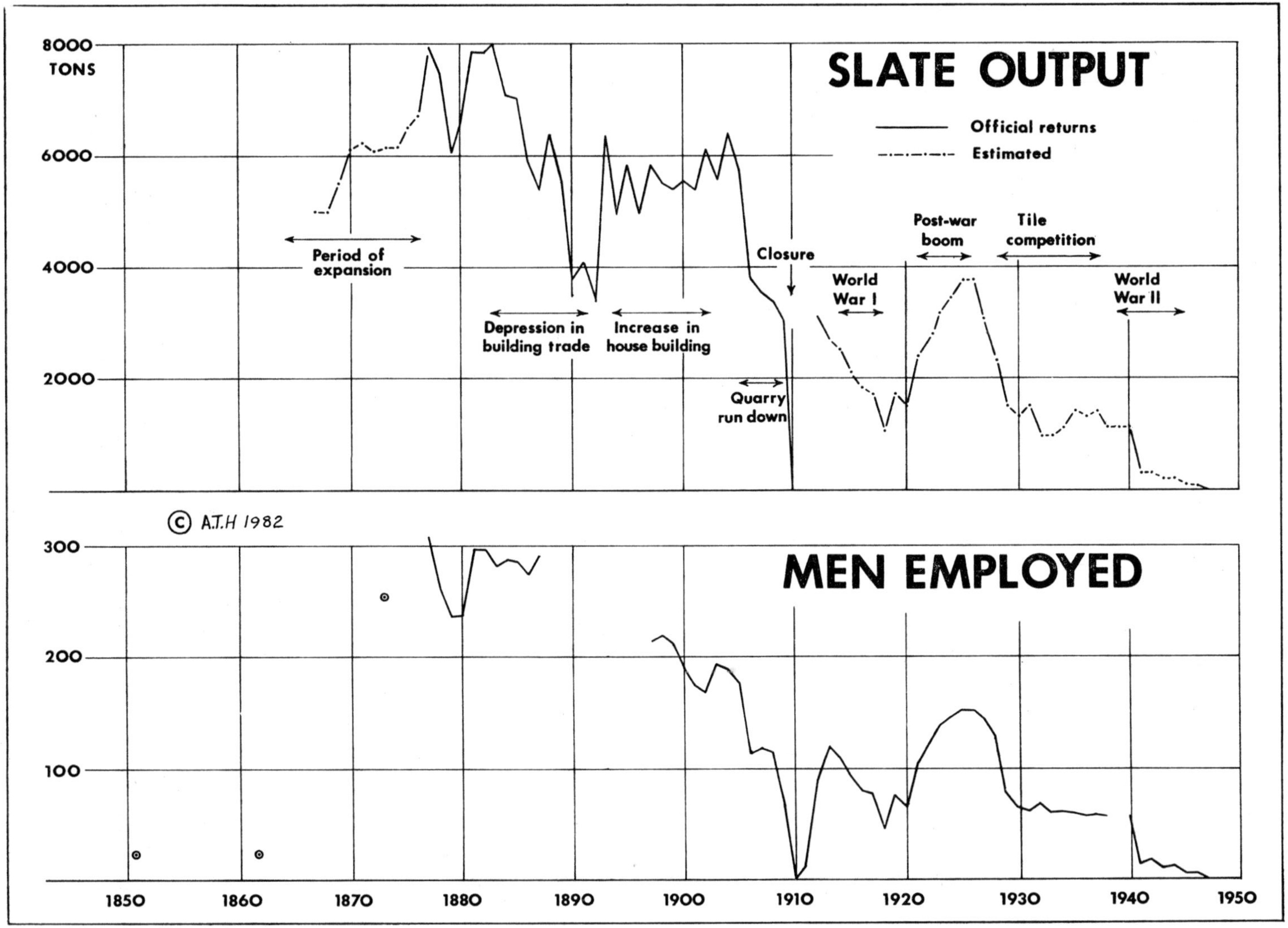
SLATE OUTPUT
Official returns
Estimated
8000
TONS
6000
4000
2000
Period of expansion
Depression in building trade
Increase in house building
Closure
Quarry run down
World War I
Post-war boom
Tile competition
World War II
© A.T.H 1982
MEN EMPLOYED
300
200
100
1850
1860
1870
1880
1890
1900
1910
1920
1930
1940
1950

Figure 10

1897-1938 and 1940-46.[12] Our interpretation of the available data is shown graphically on figure 10.

Annual output per man deduced from these sources was never high by the standards of the large quarries and averaged about 24 tons during the 1880s. It rose to 30 tons in the 1900s but this reflects the run down of development work in the closing years of McConnel's leases, and the demand during the three year lock-out at the Penrhyn Quarries in Bethesda. After the First World War there was a rise in activity but it was short-lived, and by 1930 output was little over 1,000 tons per annum. In the Second War period, production all but ceased. After 1910 the average annual output per man employed probably never reached twenty tons.

Accidents

Slate quarries were always potentially dangerous places to work in and Bryneglwys certainly claimed its toll of life and limb. We know of 20 fatalities and there were doubtless others in the years before official returns were made. The two commonest causes of fatal accidents were falling down shafts and being crushed by falling rock. Official returns were not kept before 1875, but a newspaper report of July 1866 records the death of a Bryneglwys quarryman named Owen who died after a fall.[13] A summary of known fatal accidents is given in the table in Appendix 1.

The worst year in the returns is 1877 with four fatalities in the quarry and another on the exit tramway when a man died after being thrown from a truck in which he was riding illegally down an incline. On 7 December, David Evans, 38 and Hugh Jones, 27, miners, were found dead after being crushed by a large piece of stone which had slid down from the face of the rock where they had been working. Their bodies were discovered by another workman who passed through their chamber and noticed that a blast had recently gone off, and that their candle had fallen.

> Assistance was at once obtained and the bodies released. The remains of one of the men were so mutilated that they had to be collected into a kind of sack for removal. Both men were married, one with six and the other with four children.[14]

The inquest jury returned a verdict of 'Accidentally killed by the falling of a stone at Bryneglwys Quarry'.

Another miner, Edward Davies, died by falling from the Narrow Vein landing stage whilst he and another man were unhooking the lifting chains from a wagon. His partner said that he saw Davies fall headfirst down the shaft, and supposed that the suspension chain swung violently whilst he was handling the hook, throwing him off balance. The Mines Inspector commented in his report that:

[12] Home Office (later Board of Trade), List of Mines, published annually.
[13] *Merionethshire Standard and Mid Wales Herald,* 14 July 1866.
[14] *Cambrian News,* 14 and 21 December 1877.

> the method of drawing and landing stuff in this place is one seen in slate mines and quarries only and is to my mind far from being safe or satisfactory, but as it has become general throughout the slate producing districts of Wales it would probably not be easy to obtain its disuse.[15]

An insecure chain led to the death of Owen Ellis, a 42-year old rockman on 28 February 1894. A slate block was being lowered from one underground floor to another by means of a winch and chain when it became lodged part way down against a step in the rockface. Ellis decided to climb down and release it with a crowbar, using a chain to support his weight. The chain was attached to an iron peg driven into the rock. Whilst climbing down, he appeared to lose control and fell to the floor below where he received fractures to the skull, spinal column and ribs. He died shortly afterwards, and the inquest which was held at the Railway Inn was attended by Dr. LeNeve Foster, H.M. Inspector of Mines.[16] He questioned one witness who stated that he believed the block to have come into contact with Ellis's chain, damaging the fastening. The verdict was death from injuries accidentally received.

The average annual death rate at Bryneglwys from 1875 to 1884 was 2.22 per thousand employees, this rate rising to 2.4 in the following decade and easing to 2 in 1895-1904. These figures are, on average, typical of slate mines for the period. There were no fatalities reported in 1905-14, after which the official returns ceased. We know of two deaths in the quarry between 1914 and the closure, and if this is the total then the rate was about half that in the preceding forty years.

There were many cases of non-fatal injuries, from bruises to broken bones. In a two-year period from the end of 1896 the local newspaper reported ten accidents at the quarry, doubtless a small proportion of the total number.[17] Again, rock falls and slipping over ledges and shafts accounted for many injuries, but others occurred in the mills. Fingers were caught in machinery, for example in November 1896 Silvanus Pughe got his hand trapped in the gear wheels of a sawbench, and in 1898 Morgan Roberts was using a dressing machine when his hand was caught by the rotating knives.

Other accidents which feature in the reports include men falling from ladders and several cases involving shot firing. Rees Evans, a miner was badly burned about the face and eyes in 1883 when he returned to his workplace after setting light to two holes, thinking they had both exploded together. In fact one hole had hung fire and went off a few minutes after his return. In other cases injuries and prosecutions followed when charges which had failed to fire were illegally bored out.

Quarrymen who were disabled as a result of injuries received at work had to go 'on the parish' for relief, for example in 1878 there were twenty-eight people listed as paupers through accidents in slate quarries in the parish of Llanfihangel-

15 Report of the Inspector of Mines, North Wales District, 1877.
16 *Cambrian News,* 9 March 1894.
17 *Towyn-on-Sea and Merioneth County Times.* Bound volumes in Tywyn Public Library, 1896-8.

y-Pennant.[18] The incidence of paupers amongst the population dependent upon quarries for their sustenance was nearly twice as high, in percentage terms, as amongst the agricultural population in the Talyllyn District.

The attitudes of managers and men towards safety were revealed at the Slate Mines Enquiry in 1894.[19] Meyrick Roberts was questioned by the chairman, LeNeve Foster, about the rockfall which killed David Evans and Hugh Jones in 1877:

> Were they in charge of the rock that fell on them?
> No.
> Therefore it could not have been their fault?
> No, except that they did not inspect the place above them before they began to work. They ought to have done that.
> Do you inspect these places often?
> What places?
> The places you have left.
> We do not inspect them, but the men inspect for themselves, and if they think there is anything dangerous we go there at once. They must tell us about it first.
> But you do not go yourself?
> No, we have no regular system of inspection.
> Where a place goes out of the man's reach you do not inspect those places?
> No.
> Do you not think it would be better to inspect it periodically — do you think it would reduce the number of accidents?
> I do not know.

Later, the committee questioned Hugh Roberts, a rockman, on the cause of accidents:

> If I understand you rightly, you say that a great majority of the accidents happen through carelessness on the part of the men, who are anxious to make wages?
> Yes, my experience is that at least three out of every four accidents, if not the whole of them, occur through over-haste or over-anxiety on the part of the men to make wages.
> Do you find that to be a great temptation to the men?
> Yes it is, to those who get rather small wages.

The health of the quarrymen, particularly those working in the dust caused by the saws in the mills but also those subjected to the smoke and dust following underground blasting, suffered from respiratory diseases. For many years the link between dust and disease was not officially recognised, and as late as 1922 the Medical Officer at Penrhyn claimed that slate dust was not merely harmless but beneficial. In 1939 slate mines were included under the silicosis scheme of the Workmen's Compensation Acts. This was extended to include shed-workers in open quarries in 1946.

Mrs. Roberts of Abergynolwyn tells how she lost her father at Bryneglwys in 1928:

[18] *Carnarvon and Denbigh Herald,* 20 July 1878.
[19] Report of the Departmental Committee upon Merionethshire Slate Mines, 1895.

> My father was killed, you see, in the big hollow on the left hand side of the road going to the quarry, which you can see today. Well, he was blasting the rock there and I happened to be at home that day, although I was usually out working then, I was a teenager. It was at eleven o'clock in the morning and my mother came to the door for something (we lived at Cantrybedd) and she said 'there's something wrong at the Vaen Fawr'. She could see some men running along the road, something had happened. One man came running towards the house and she went to meet him. 'What has happened to Huw?' she said. There were several men working there but something told her that it was my father, it's very funny you know. Of course there was no first aid up there, only a few had some idea, and they couldn't stop the blood. He had been blasting and a piece of rock was standing after the blast and he went to move it, and when it was coming he ran but slipped on the rock. The stone came down on his legs. They took him down to Tywyn but it took three hours because something happened to the ambulance. He reached the hospital at two o'clock and they amputated the leg. He came round in the evening, my mother went and talked to him and then came home. She walked all the way from the village up to the house, she'd only been home about half an hour when two men came to say that he'd passed away.

Managers

We know of six managers, or agents as they were generally called, from 1849 onwards. The first of these was the Englishman George Smith from Amport, Hampshire. He lived at Bryneglwys with his wife and family in 1851, and a report on the quarry which he wrote in 1857 survives but we have discovered little else about him.

Robert Williams began to work the quarry for John Lloyd Jones in October 1862, continuing under the McConnels through the major developments of the 1860s. He was thus responsible for the works on the Narrow Vein which established twenty chambers by 1876, or so he claims in his autobiography. It is difficult to say to what extent, if any, he is to blame for the failure of the quarry to pay during this time, but when T. H. McConnel died in 1873 the Board sent James Stevens to the quarry in an attempt to retrieve the situation, much to Williams's dismay. He said in his autobiography:

> as every quarryman in every quarry in Wales knows, when an Englishman comes in as an official in a Welsh quarry he generally feels obliged to show himself to be superior at all times . . . It was rather an effort, but I did not submit to the Englishman.

In 1876 Williams accepted an offer of a post at Abercwmeiddaw Slate Quarry, but he departed soon afterwards following a dispute over the extent of his authority — with another Englishman! After retiring, he lived in Tywyn until his death in 1898 aged 85. His remains were interred in his native Llanllyfni.

Evan Evans held the post of manager for a short period, followed by Meyrick Roberts in 1880. The quarry enjoyed a period of stability following the 1881 sale, under his superintendence, and he became a well-known figure in local affairs. He was a J.P. and chairman of Abergynolwyn Parish Council. He remained until McConnel's departure in 1910.

Haydn Jones appointed David Jones as manager in 1911. He stayed until the closure of the quarry in 1920. He was replaced by R. O. Williams who had worked at Bryneglwys before but had moved to South Wales after the 1910 closure. His managership is still recalled with feeling by those who worked under him. He was said to be a stern disciplinarian, insisting on strict timekeeping and swearing freely. In short, a hard man. No doubt he was brought in by Haydn Jones to counter the agitation which had surfaced during the events which culminated in the stoppage in 1920, and in this he apparently succeeded.

3

Quarry Buildings

THE rough blocks of slate rock hewn from the quarry face were taken to the mills for processing into finished slabs or roofing slates. There were three principal mills, or cutting sheds, at Bryneglwys, the Old Mill and the New Mill on the Upper Level and the Lower Mill (Shed Isaf) on the Lower Level. Whereas it was common practice elsewhere for the slatemakers, that is the men who split the blocks into thin sheets to form roofing slates, to work in open fronted sheds ('waliau') they did not do so at Bryneglwys. They worked in the mills, under the same roof as the sawing and dressing machines.

The blocks were first cut into convenient sized pieces, which for roofing slates meant about 3 inches (75 mm) thick and roughly rectangular in shape. The slatemaker used a broad bladed chisel and a wooden mallet to split the blocks into sheets down to about one-fifth of an inch (5 mm) thick, an operation requiring great skill which was only acquired after long experience. Boys learned their craft under the eye of older relatives in the quarry; Mr. Caradog Jones relates his early years there:

> I started work in July 1918 when I was 13 years of age. There were very few working there then, mainly elderly quarrymen and I started as a saw sharpener, earning two shillings (10p) a day. Every chance I had I used to learn splitting and dressing slates. After six months I became a learner splitter and dresser but the trouble was we had to learn on spare bits of rock. You couldn't earn much money on that business because the men that worked the chambers always took everything for themselves so you only had the scraps. The make at the end of the month was about a thousand damp-course slates and the price was 2½d (1p) a hundred. But in every hundred you counted 155 slates to allow for breakages, so you can imagine what the wages of a learner were in those days — it could be about 7/6d (37½p) a month. Nevertheless we managed and the community of Abergynolwyn was quite a happy one under the circumstances, for the simple reason that we didn't know any other way, we lived here and were brought up here and were quite content.

After splitting, the slates were trimmed to standard sizes with a hand-knife (cyllell naddu) or on a dressing machine. For hand dressing the slate was supported on a 'trafal', a long iron blade fixed to a wooden base, the knife being brought down in a chopping action to remove the surplus. There were two types of dressing machine used at Bryneglwys. The 'injian naddu' had a rotating cutter with two knives, similar to a lawn mower cylinder, and the slate was rested on a bar in front of the cutter when being trimmed. There was a gauge fixed at right angles to the bar to ensure that the slate was cut to one of a range of standard sizes. It consisted simply of a metal bar with notches on the upper surface to locate the outer edge of the slate.

The 'injian dradlo' had a straight knife pivoted at one end, like an ordinary guillotine. The machines at Bryneglwys actually had two knives each, mounted back to back on a common shaft. They were driven from the lineshaft, fast and loose pulleys being provided to allow each machine to be engaged only when required. The reciprocating motion caused severe vibration, leading to bearing failures. They were supplied by de Winton of Caernarfon, probably the type made under Amos and Francis patent.

The Old Mill

The Old Mill was situated on the Upper Level (see figure 11) and was a rambling, complex building put together in several successive phases. The earliest room was 1, and was most probably John Pughe's mill of 1847. If so, it bore a tablet, now in Abergynolwyn Museum, inscribed *These Premises were erected by John Pughe in 1847, much to the credit of (word missing) person who bore the expense*. The inside dimensions were 48 feet long by 47 feet wide (14.6 m × 14.3 m), eaves and ridge heights being 6 feet 6 inches (2 m) and 22 feet (6.7 m) respectively. The gable walls were of thin irregular blocks with few if any sawn ends. The side walls had been much altered, the window openings near the S.W. and N.E. corners having been subsequently filled in. Little of the original masonry remained in the side walls, which had two openings for tramways. We found some parts of roof trusses, containing rough hewn timber and showing signs of much repair and strengthening over the years. The east wall had a massive stone buttress built against it on the inside, the wall bulging inwards by at least a foot at the top.

Pughe erected his mill close by the Cantrybedd bank of the Boundary Stream and the obvious inference is that he intended to drive the machinery by a water wheel, though he made no reference to this in his *Mining Journal* notice. There is no trace of a wheelpit, although the site where one would expect to find it was occupied by the smithy. There were lineshaft bearings in both gable walls, but they were bedded on sawn blocks which had clearly been added later. The machinery installed in the mill probably consisted of saws and planers used for making slabs. A hand driven saw has been found at a nearby quarry and it is likely that Pughe depended on manual power for driving the machinery.

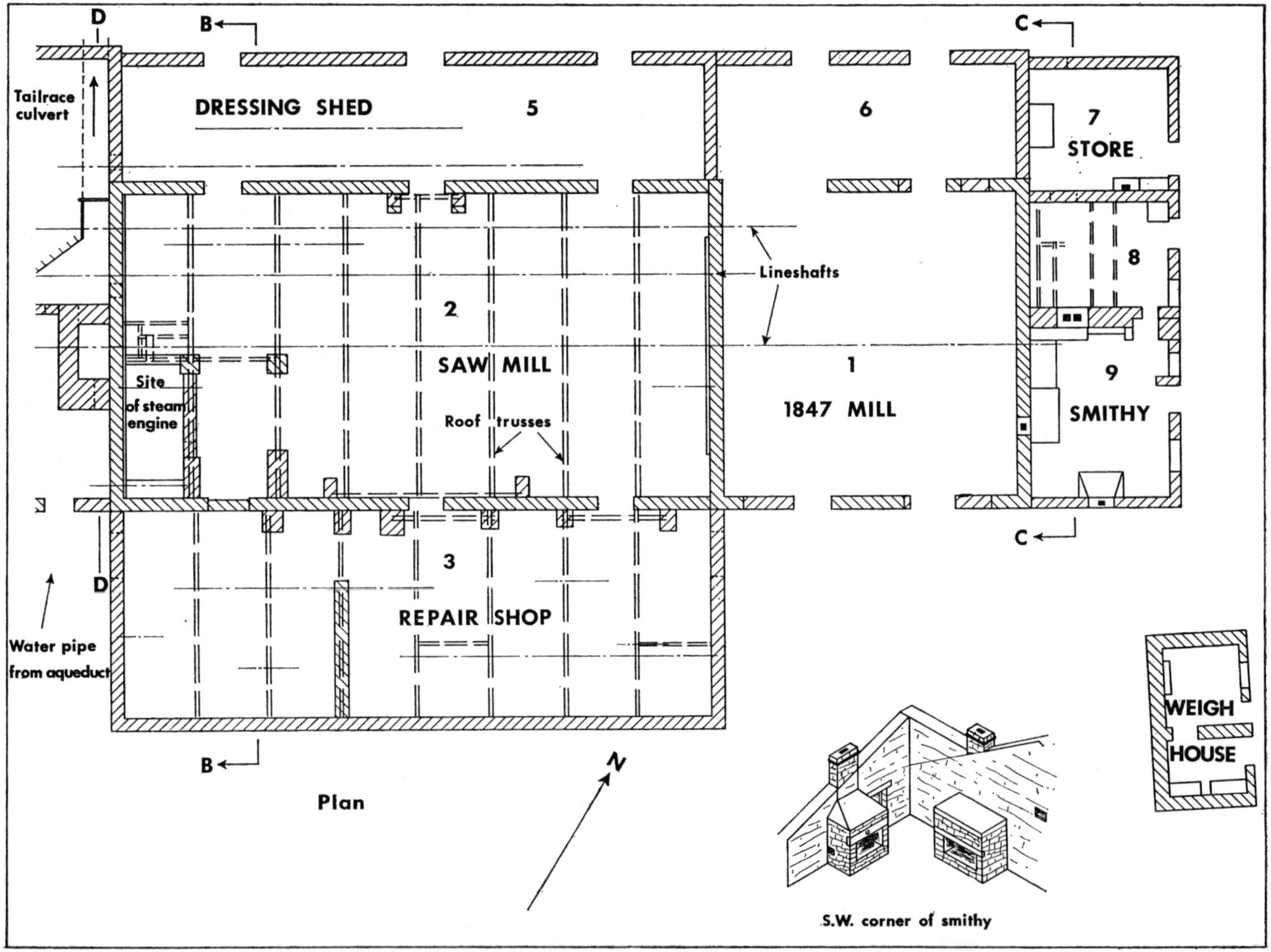
D
B
C
Tailrace culvert
DRESSING SHED
5
6
7
STORE
8
9
SMITHY
2
SAW MILL
Site of steam engine
Roof trusses
Lineshafts
1
1847 MILL
3
REPAIR SHOP
Water pipe from aqueduct
N
WEIGH HOUSE
Plan
S.W. corner of smithy

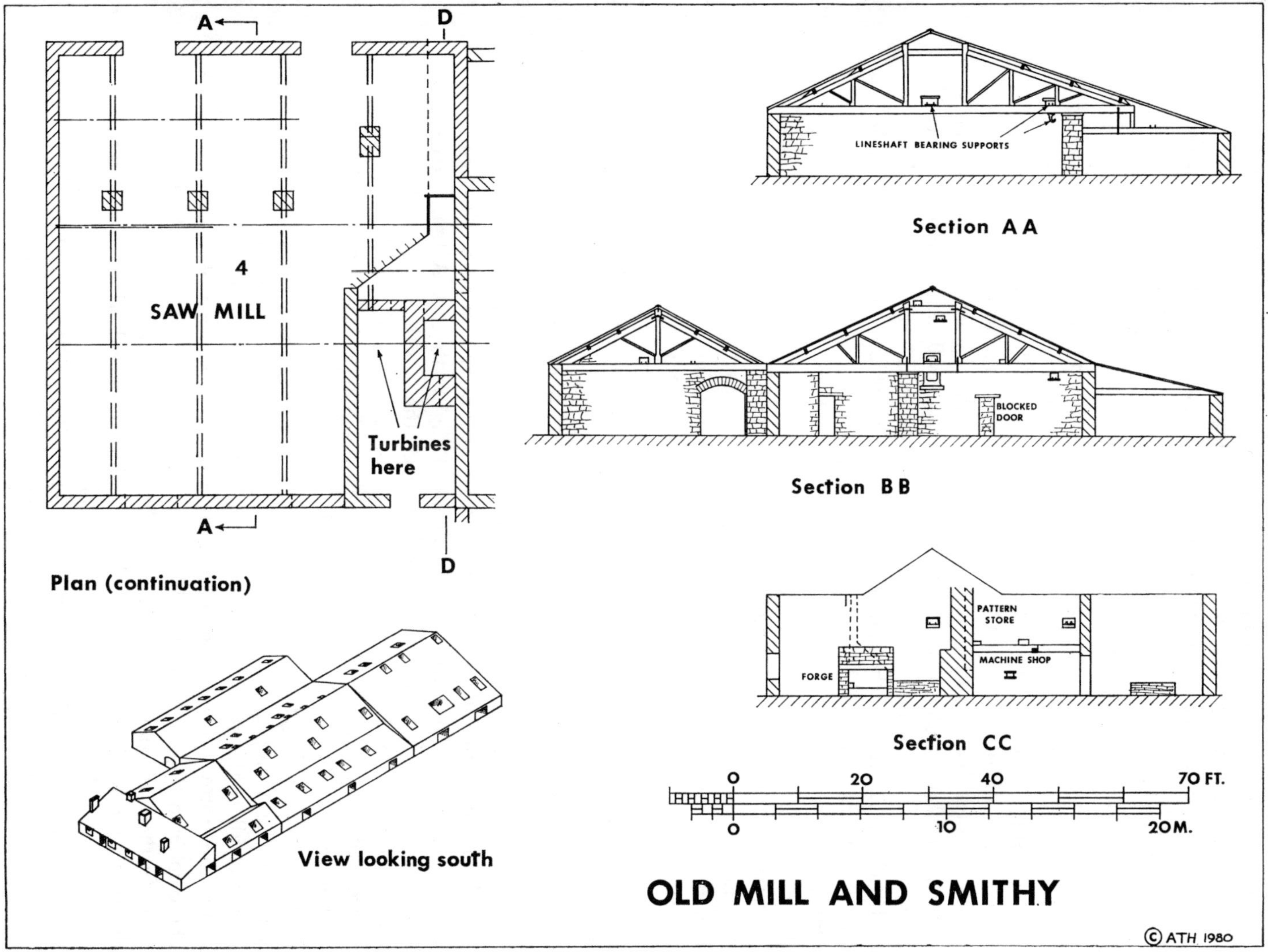
A
D
4
SAW MILL
Turbines here
A
D
Plan (continuation)
View looking south
LINESHAFT BEARING SUPPORTS
Section AA
BLOCKED DOOR
Section BB
PATTERN STORE
MACHINE SHOP
FORGE
Section CC
0
20
40
70 FT.
0
10
20 M.
OLD MILL AND SMITHY
© ATH 1980

Figure 11

The next phase of development consisted of an extension on the west end of the mill, room 2. It was 88 feet long (16.8 m) inside and as the side walls were higher than those of room 1 the common gable wall had to be built up to fit the roofline of the new room. There were three doorways in each side wall, with slate lintels, and the construction was in rough slab with some sawn ends. The mill was typical of those of its day, and originally there would have been six sets of machinery, saw tables and dressing machines, served by tramways laid across the building through the doorways. There were seven timber roof trusses which also supported the main shafting running along the centre of the mill, and at least four other lineshafts, some by underslung bearings carried on J-shaped castings. The shafting was altered during the life of the mill, as was the machinery layout. A curious feature of the north wall was a series of five narrow vertical slits which were built into the original wall, but were later filled in with slab. It is likely that room 2 was built during John Lloyd Jones's tenure of the quarry in 1862-3.

Outside the west end of room 2 there was a roofed extension, open to the north, enclosing a waterwheel (or turbine) to drive the mill machinery. The space was 15 feet (4.47 m) wide, far greater than would be needed for a conventional overshot wheel, and we do not know what type was used.

The next phase of construction, in the mid-1860s, involved a considerable extension of the mill. At the west end, room 4 was added, 67 feet wide by 60 feet long (20.4 m × 18.3 m) enclosing the waterwheel pit. The south wall, which was in line with that of room 2, contained two elegant arched doorways, identical in style to the ones in Pendre locomotive shed on the Talyllyn Railway. The north wall was some 20 feet (6.1 m) forward of the room 2 building line and had two plain rectangular doorways opposite the arched ones. The roof was asymmetrical and to match its profile the gable wall of room 2 had to be raised on the north side. There were three timber trusses of 43 feet 6 inches (13.3 m) clear span supported on slab pillars at the north end. A fourth truss spanned the space between the wheelpit and the north wall. A lean-to extension, 5, was added to room 2 and a span-roof room, 6, was built on to the north side of room 1. The span-roof was necessary because the eaves of room 1 were only 6 feet 6 inches (2 m) high.

Room 3 was a large span-roof building on the south side of room 2. Because of the rising ground behind 2, a fair amount of excavation was necessary to allow this to be accommodated. The gable walls had arched doorways for the tramways, of a different pattern to those in room 4.

The combined floor area of the mill was about 17,500 square feet (1,627 m^2) and no further additions were made to it, although detail alterations were made from time to time such as blocking-up doorways and window openings. Some walls were buttressed to counteract subsidence and several roof trusses had makeshift supports of timbers laid on piers built against the walls.

The tramways in the the mill were planned to form a merry-go-round system for delivering slabs to the machine rooms. Loaded wagons from the quarry arrived at the weigh-house, where each load would be checked, and then run via a turntable along a line laid outside the mill next to the south wall. This line passed through room 3 and had turntables containing the tracks running into the mill. After the slabs were unloaded alongside the machines, the empty wagons could be taken out and returned to the quarry via a line laid outside the north wall of the mill. This line also served the slate yard, where finished slates and slabs were stored awaiting shipment to Tywyn. It was a continuation of the exit tramway. The track along the south side was later shortened and the archways in room 4 blocked-up, probably when the quarry output fell and parts of the mill became disused.

The saw tables and planers were situated in the larger rooms, each sawing machine consisted of a long bedplate supporting a table which travelled back and forth on slides. The circular saw blade was mounted on a horizontal arbor carried on the bedplate, the blade projecting up through a slot in the table, to which the slate blocks were fixed by chains and wedges. The saw blades needed frequent sharpening once or even twice daily, and there were machines provided specially for this purpose. We found a quantity of saw sharpening files in room 2 during our survey. Slabs which needed flat surfaces, such as billiard tables, headstones, etc., were machined on planers which were similar in principle to those used to machine metal in engineering workshops. The slab was secured to the table of the planer, which travelled back and forth beneath a fixed cutting tool. After each cut the tool was traversed a small distance by a leadscrew, until the whole face of the slab was planed.

Dressers of the guillotine type were sited in rooms 5 and 6. Rubbish arising from the machine rooms was loaded into wagons running on tracks laid below the floor level, and run out to the tips via tunnels under the slate yard. Some slate offcuts however were used as building material. Many of the quarry buildings themselves contained pieces which showed the marks of the saw teeth on the exposed edge, and the pieces cut from the long edges of the blocks found a use for fencing. Many of these slate fences survive, each piece being driven into the ground and the tops held between two interwoven wires.

The machines were driven by belt and pulley from lineshafting running the entire length of the mill. The shafting layout shown on the plan has been inferred from our survey of the decaying remains of the beams. The men worked by daylight in the mills, the roof lights being glazed with half-inch (12 mm) thick panes. When the saws were operating, the atmosphere was laden with fine slate dust. There was no forced ventilation, a water dip for each saw blade being the only attempt made to lay the deadly dust. Otherwise, it could only escape through the shed doorways, when they were opened.

The development of the water power used to drive the mill machinery is problematical, several major alterations having been made, but turbines were certainly used from an early date. A walled pit was built against the outside of the west wall of room 2, extending up to the roof ridge. This was fed by a wooden launder carried on A-shaped supports, and within the pit there was, probably, a vertical axis reaction turbine. This type of machine ran with a draft tube whose lower end was submerged in the tailrace channel, and was fed by a vertical pipe from the launder. The masonry within the pit had been chased to accommodate the pipe, and some of the supporting ragbolts were found *in situ*. The effective hydraulic head was approximately 20 feet (6 m) and the drive to the lineshaft would have been by bevel gears.

A later development involved the removal of the vertical axis machine, probably in 1910 and its replacement by an impulse turbine. The water supply came from the small reservoir along an aqueduct carried on a slab embankment at a higher level than the old launder, giving about 40 feet (12 m) head with an iron pipe laid down a sloping ramp into the mill. Openings were cut through the wall of the turbine pit to allow the pipe to enter, and for easy access to the machinery. A 16½ h.p. 12 inch Turgo impulse turbine was supplied by Gilbert Gilkes of Kendal in August 1923, but it is not known where it was installed.

To provide steam power when the water supply failed, a boiler was installed in the west end of room 3, which was partitioned off by a slab wall. Another space was walled off in room 2 for a steam engine, and the main lineshaft bearing in the gable wall above was supported on a massive cast iron box set into the masonry. There must have been a floor laid at truss beam level over the engine room, judging by two pockets in the wall with studs for bearing pedestals, suggesting that there was a small workshop up there.

Smithy and machine shop

There was a three-roomed lean-to structure against the east gable wall of the mill, the wall being raised to a uniform height of 15 feet 6 inches (4.73 m) to support the roof. Here were sited the smithy, machine shop and stores. The blacksmiths and fitters held important positions in the quarry, being responsible for maintaining all things mechanical in good repair. Mill machinery, lifting gear, waterwheels and wagons had to be kept in working order and all but major repairs were done on site. A wide variety of replacement parts came from the blacksmith's forge and anvil, bearings were remetalled and small iron castings were almost certainly poured there.

In room 9 there were originally four hearths. The two built against the south and west walls had manual bellows but the one on the north wall may have had a blower driven from the lineshaft. The fourth hearth had become redundant and was cut through to make a doorway into room 8, which was a fitting shop with a pattern loft above. The inventory included a lathe and doubtless a pillar drill and a screwcutting machine. Two pieces of TR rail bent into an L-shape, one leg grouted into the wall and the other buried in the floor, acted as supports for a sturdy bench. There was a window above the bench but it had been blocked up, probably when room 7 was added on. We found many wooden patterns amongst the debris in room 8, mostly bearing brasses and other small components. There was a small hearth, probably used for tinsmith work, in the north-east corner.

Rooms 8 and 9 were built of irregular slate slabs with some sawn pieces and

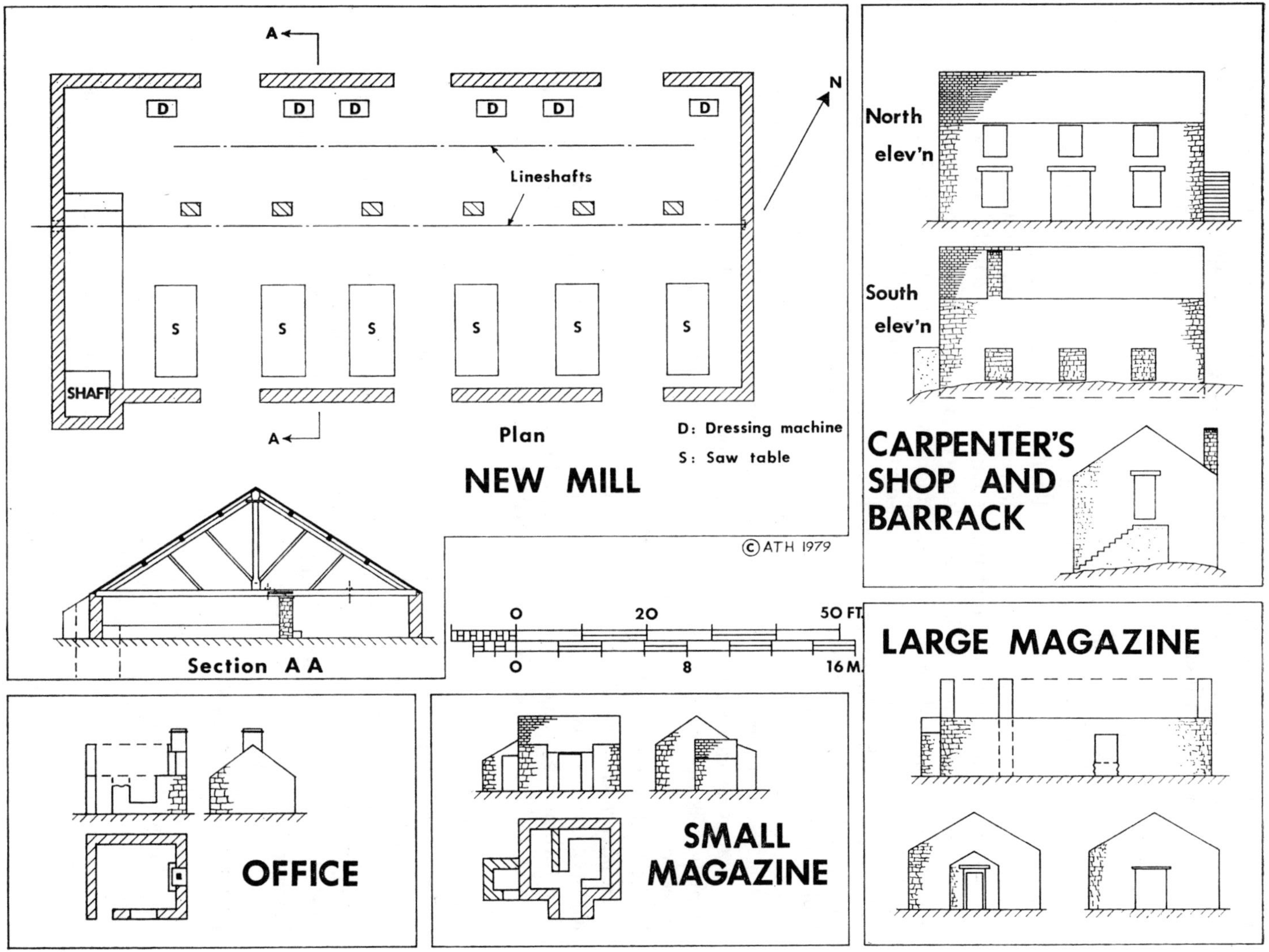
A
A
N
D
D
D
D
D
D
Lineshafts
S
S
S
S
S
S
SHAFT
Plan
NEW MILL
D: Dressing machine
S: Saw table
Section A A
©ATH 1979
0
20
50 FT.
0
8
16 M.
North
elev'n
South
elev'n
CARPENTER'S
SHOP AND
BARRACK
LARGE MAGAZINE
OFFICE
SMALL
MAGAZINE

Figure 12

were most probably contemporary with room 2. Room 7 was of sawn, squared slabs and must have been a later addition. There were no lineshafts in 7, and it seems to have been used as a store.

New Mill

The building was a simple rectangular span-roof structure whose most remarkable feature was the mouth of a shaft within the south-east corner, leading vertically down to the Long Tunnel. The mill, shown on figure 12, was otherwise conventional, somewhat larger than room 2 of the Old Mill but having a similar layout. The roof trusses had main beams 12 inches by 8 inches (300 mm × 200 mm) which were formed of two lengths joined near the centre and supported on slab pillars under the joints. The main lineshaft ran the full length of the mill, slightly off-centre, and projected through the east gable wall. Another shaft was supported on each truss beam but did not extend to the end walls. There would have been six sawing machines in the southern half of the mill and dressers on the other side.

The machinery was driven latterly by a turbine installed on a platform some 20 feet (6 m) down the shaft. An earlier drive arrangement shown on the 1887 OS plan was carried on a row of pillars between the Old and New Mills, though it is not clear whether they supported a lanuder leading to a water-wheel or a shaft drive between the mills. Since there is no trace of a wheelpit in the field or on the plan, a shaft drive or flat-rods seems more likely.

In later years the mill ceased to be used for its original purpose and it became a storeroom for hay, etc., and also a meeting room where concerts were held. The turbine was removed from the shaft in the 1920s, a task vividly recalled by Mr. Griffith Evans who was lowered on a rope to dismantle it.

Carpenters shop

This was originally a single storey span-roof building 40 feet 6 inches (12.3 m) long, having a large entrance doorway wide enough for a tramway, though none is marked on the OS plans. It had two large windows at the front and originally three at the rear, alhough they had been blocked up as the waste tips advanced towards the building. An upper floor was added later to form a barrack.

Weigh-house and office

This was a two-roomed span-roof building 27 feet long by 15 feet 6 inches wide (8.23 m × 4.73 m). The weighbridge was situated on the tramway between the Daylight Adit and the Old Mill, the weigh-house occupying the room nearest the Adit. The other room was an office. On the gable wall at the office end hung the quarry bell which summoned generations of men to their work. Caradog Jones describes how

> We started work at seven o'clock in the morning and we had to be on the right side of the boundary wall when the bell stopped, otherwise you'd be

View of the Upper Level taken in 1958. The Narrow Vein workings lie across the valley on the left; the tips in the centre consist of waste rock hauled up by the large water wheels. The Barracks. Weighhouse, Smithy and Mills were still largely intact and the hillside has been planted with trees. The group of fir trees, including a monkey-puzzle, planted in the 1860s stands behind the New Mill.

(Author)

Another view in 1958, showing the main Barracks in the foreground and the Carpenter's Shop and Barracks with external staircase on the right. Beyond the windowless Magazine is the Manager's house with the quarry office adjoining. The row of pillars, centre right, carried a launder to the waterwheel behind the hut containing the winding drum used for haulage from Chamber 8B.

(Author)

The Old and New Mills about six years after closure, after removal of the tramway rails and other ironwork for scrap. Bryneglwys Farm, partly unroofed, is the group of buildings to the left of the Manager's house.

(J. Adams)

A group posed outside the Lower Mill. Note the horse, Beudynewydd Incline just visible on the left, and the roof of Beudybach Cottage, later buried beneath the waste tips.

(Caradog Jones collection)

Slatemaking and dressing in the Lower Mill.

(Caradog Jones collection)

The Lower Mill in 1958. The front wall is heavily buttressed following the landslide which demolished a 90ft. long section to the right of the surviving portion.

(Author)

'Savoy Cafe', the messroom or caban by the Lower Mill.

(Author)

A brace of slate wagons in Nant Gwernol after a runaway on Cantrybedd Incline.

(Author)

> on the carpet with the manager; but the old bellringer was always looking towards the road and if he could see one of us coming he'd keep on ringing till we were inside the wall.

We found traces of an earlier lean-to roof, indicating rebuilding at some time. An early photograph shows the barracks and smithy in final form but the weigh-house has the lean-to roof.

Magazines

The large Magazine was 41 feet 6 inches long × 20 feet wide (12.7 m × 6.2 m) excluding the entrance porch at the east end. An internal doorless wall divided the building into two rooms, the larger one having had a tramway laid in. The porch, which led to the smaller room, had a double entrance with narrow doorways. Kegs of black powder were kept in the large room and high explosive for the miners in the other. A special gunpowder van brought the explosives in via the Exit Tramway and the Talyllyn Railway from Tywyn Wharf.

A smaller magazine, also having two rooms, was sited some 200 yards (183 m) north of the Old Mill. The single-entrance led via a porch into the larger room which had a slab bench around the walls. The roof was lined with timber when surveyed, in accordance with regulations requiring powder magazines to be so fitted to prevent any risk of sparks. There was a small lean-to shed against the south wall, apparently a privy.

Between this magazine and the Old Mill lay a small building containing a fireplace and plastered walls. It served latterly as a 'caban'.

Lower Mill

In its final form this must have been one of the longest sheds in the slate industry, see figure 13. It was sited on levelled ground formed from rock waste brought out of the Long Tunnel. McConnel evidently followed his outright purchase of the quarry in 1881 by erecting the first portion of the building, consisting of a mill 155 feet 9 inches long × 36 feet wide inside (47.4 m × 11 m) plus a smithy and stable at the east end. Above the stable door was a stone tablet inscribed *W. H. McCONNEL ESqR. 1881 M.R. MANAGER* (M.R. was Meyrick Roberts). The end wall contained a blocked up window and the wall laid with small slabs set on edge. There was a hearth in the smithy against the south wall.

The mill had tramway entrances along the north wall only, with sliding wooden double doors on each. The roof trusses supported two lineshafts running the length of the mill, the drive turbine being sited in an enclosed area at the west end of the building. The turbine was of the impulse type, the water supply coming from the Boundary Reservoir. There was an opening in the rear wall of the mill where the pipe came through. A piece of cast iron pipe of 5 inch bore (127 mm) was found, which may have been part of the turbine supply pipe. The tailrace culvert was laid from the turbine house under the floor

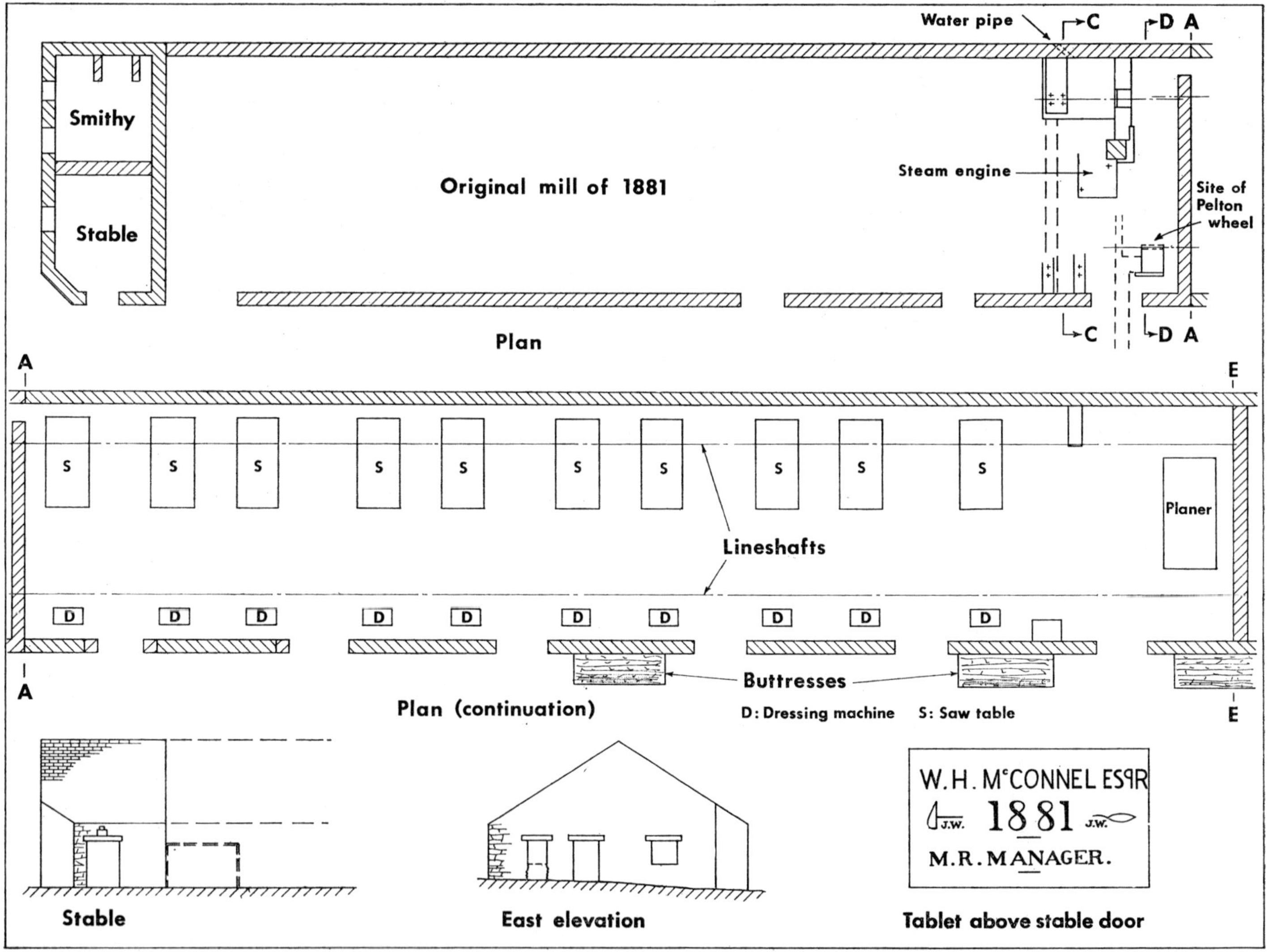

Water pipe
C
D
A
Smithy
Stable
Original mill of 1881
Steam engine
Site of Pelton wheel
Plan
E
S
Planer
Lineshafts
D
Buttresses
Plan (continuation)
D: Dressing machine
S: Saw table
Stable
East elevation
W.H. McCONNEL ESQR
J.W. 1881 J.W.
M.R. MANAGER.
Tablet above stable door

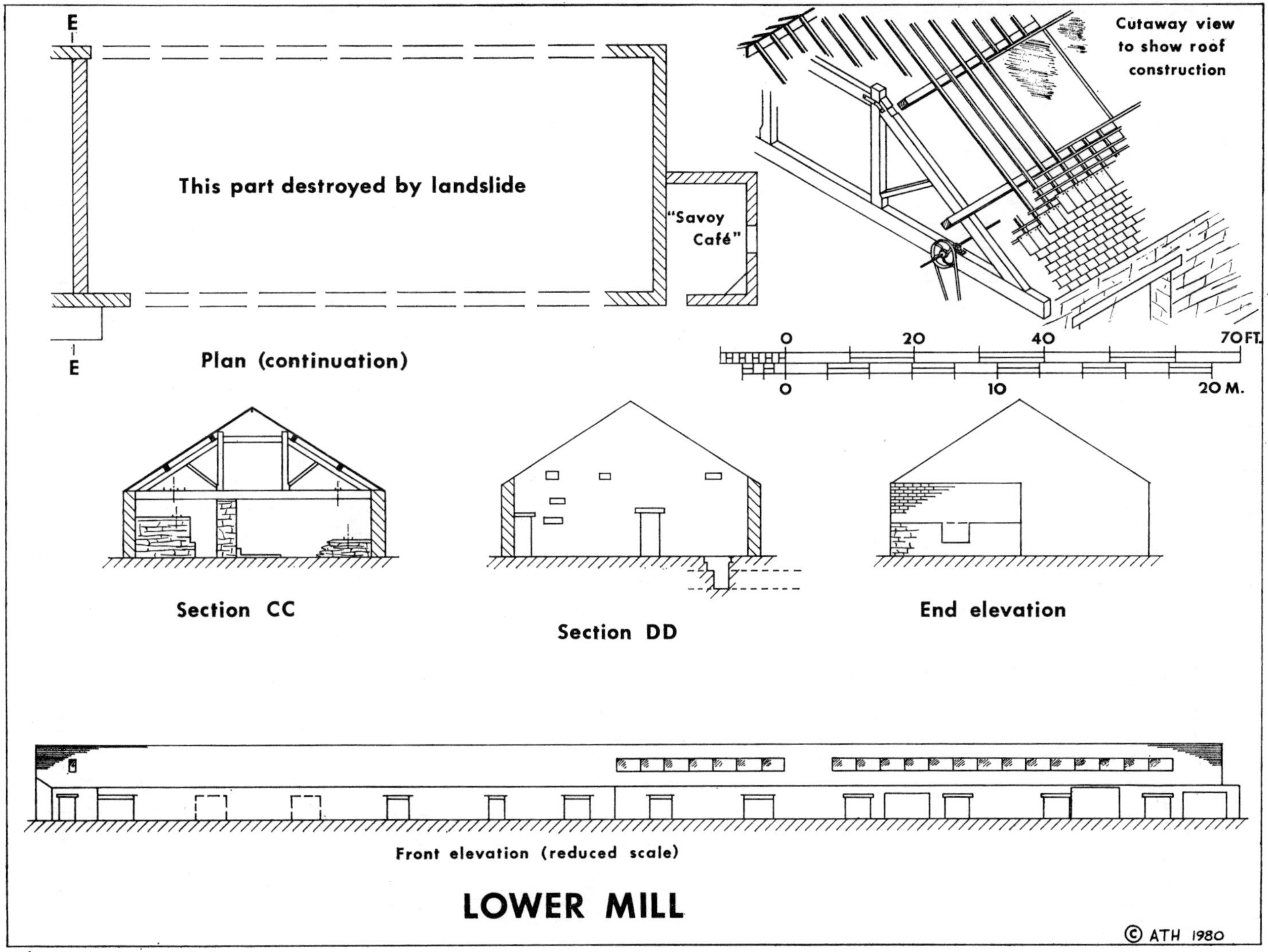
E
E
This part destroyed by landslide
"Savoy Café"
Plan (continuation)
Cutaway view to show roof construction
0
20
40
70FT.
0
10
20 M.
Section CC
Section DD
End elevation
Front elevation (reduced scale)
LOWER MILL
© ATH 1980

Figure 13

in a direct line to the river, and is made of slab walling covered over with large slabs.

A steel hoop 19½ inches (495 mm) internal diameter was found attached to the roof truss above the turbine room. This is believed to have supported the chimney of a boiler used to supply a steam engine, in this case a portable type. It was used to drive the machinery when the water supply failed, and reputedly was removed at about the time of the First World War.

The mill was greatly extended in the years prior to 1901, the new room making the overall length of the building 452 feet (137.8 m). Power was transmitted by two lineshafts running the full length of the new section, which was identical in construction to the original part. Sometime in the early 1930s a landslide on the hillside above the mill demolished a large portion of the new section at the west end. A new transverse wall was built 88 feet (26.8 m) from the end, and the front wall of the remaining portion was buttressed against further subsidence. After closure the TR Co. took a considerable quantity of slab from the derelict mill for use on the Nant Gwernol extension works.

A small lean-to shed against the original west wall was a caban or mess-room for the men. The words '*Savoy Cafe*' were carved into the lintel over the entrance, and the same title was pecked into the wood of the door. Inside, there was a homely fireplace with an iron grate and a neatly made slate hood above.

One of the most impressive features of the mills was the roof trusses. The construction was massive, with main beams up to 15 inches × 8 inches (380 mm × 203 mm) cross section and 50 feet (15.9 m) long. Each truss member was fitted to the next by mortice and tenon joints, reinforced with a variety of ironwork. In some cases a U-shaped metal strip was fitted around the joint and secured by iron wedges, whilst others had bolts fitted within the joint. A prodigious quantity of timber went into the Lower Mill — 27 trusses of 36 feet (11 m) clear span, containing in all 1,470 cubic feet (41.7 m^3 of wood, about 30 tons. There was as much again in the purlins, rafters and battens of the complete building. It was doubtless imported via Aberdovey which had a considerable trade in timber for the local shipbuilding industry in the nineteenth century, and all brought to the quarry along the tramway. In the New Mill the beams are at a relatively low height and it was the custom for young quarrymen to show their prowess by jumping from the floor and kicking the beams with one foot! In the dereliction period a generation of campers warmed to fires fuelled by this bounteous supply of firewood.

Other buildings on the Lower Level

There was a small building, possibly a checker's hut or office, alongside the tramway from the Long Tunnel near the Lower Mill. It has virtually disappeared due to erosion of the river bank where it stood. Near Cantrybedd Cottages stood a weigh-house and another small hut alongside the tramway between the cottages and the mill. There was a cluster of small crudely built huts on the tips opposite the cottages, but these were undoubtedly pigsties and other domestic offices.

4

Reservoirs and Aqueducts

WATER provided the energy source for driving the lifting gear, air compressors and mill machinery in the quarry. Although supplemented for a time by steam engines in times of drought, it never gave way to more modern sources of power and electricity was never used at Bryneglwys. The two main waters draining the valley, the Llaeron and Boundary streams, were both diverted and dammed in several places, altering their courses considerably over the years. To ensure regular water supplies even during drought, the reservoirs provided storage capacity though not always enough in very dry summers. A network of artificial watercourses led the precious fluid to the various parts of the quarry where it was needed. The Boundary Stream originally flowed across the Narrow Vein between chambers 1B and 1C and then past the site of the Old Mill, joining the Llaeron near the entrance to the Long Tunnel. The combined streams plus a few small tributaries form the River Gwernol.

There were several types of man-made watercourses. Some were simply ditches or leats dug into the ground and the spoil laid alongside to form raised banks. Where the soil was loose or soft the banks were lined with slabs set on edge, or smaller pieces laid in courses. This method was also used when the banks were raised above ground level, the soil being piled up outside the slabs. Another variety had the floor and sides built of rectangular slabs forming a flume, typically 2 feet 6 inches (760 mm) wide laid either on the ground or on an embankment to ensure the correct level. Timber flumes were also used, having transverse decking planks nailed to longitudinals each side to form a trough. Where the water had to flow beneath a tip it was usually culverted. The sides of the cuverts were of slabs laid in courses, and the roof consisted of large slabs laid across the top. Leats were carefully aligned relative to the slope of the ground to maintain an even gradient. Wherever possible, water discharged from a wheelpit was led to the headrace of another wheel at a lower level, as for example the Old Mill turbine which was at one time fed from the tailrace of the Narrow Vein haulage wheels.

The earliest artificial watercourses that we can identify are leats 1 and 2, figure 3. They diverted water from the Llaeron and Boundary Streams respectively, converging at a point near the Narrow Vein haulage wheels, and from there a slab flume laid part on an embankment and part on slab pillars fed the headraces. From the junction of leats 1 and 2 a leat 3 ran down to the Llaeron so that water could be diverted away from the haulage wheels when not required to drive them. The tailraces discharged into the Boundary Stream, but a sluice allowed water to be diverted via leat 4 into a small pond or forebay, still traceable, which fed a launder to the Old Mill. The launder was supported by two slab pillars which survive. The haulage wheel tailrace channels were culverted as the waste tips advanced, and the sluice was replaced by another one further downstream.

Boundary Reservoir

The original supply system for the haulage wheels proved unsatisfactory since there was no storage capacity, so in 1865-6 the Boundary Reservoir was built. The stream was dammed just above the Narrow Vein. The dam is of earth faced with slabs on the water side inclined at 35 degrees to the horizontal, topped by a vertical wall 3 feet (.91 m) high. In plan it consists of two straight portions inclined at 135 degrees to each other and the soil infill is 45 feet (13.7 m) wide at the top, sloping at 25 degrees on the air side. The dam looks as though it was built in a hurry, as the stone facing is crude and the dam cross-section varies considerably, so the above dimensions are approximate. The surface area of the water was .624 acres (.253 ha.) and it lay on the original course of the stream, which was diverted above the reservoir, a sluice controlling the flow into it. The diversion channel or spillway was cut above the east bank of the stream to allow it to bypass the dam during construction, and to enable the reservoir to be emptied for maintenance on the valves, etc. After passing the dam, the spillway narrowed and may have contained a weir, then it opened out to a wide gully before joining leat 2. There was an overflow channel at the same end of the dam, paved with slabs set on edge into the ground and dropping quite steeply down to the spillway.

The control valve was operated from a wooden staging built out from the dam. It was placed below the bed of the reservoir between two wooden poles which supported the outer end of the staging. They were 17 feet (5.2 m) high and were joined by cross-pieces to form a ladder-like frame. A catwalk 18 feet (5.5 m) long ran from the top of the dam to the frame, and the valve handwheel was mounted at the outer end. The decapitated remains of the spindle still rise from the valve buried below and part of the staging lies askew. A fragment of handwheel marked *Kendal* indicates that the supplier was Gilbert Gilkes and Gordon Ltd. or their predecessors Williamson Bros. of Kendal, Cumbria.

Construction of the reservoir meant that the Boundary Stream no longer flowed along its natural course downstream of the dam, but was diverted either onto the waterwheels or to the Llaeron via leat 3. From the valve the delivery pipe passed beneath the dam to emerge in a slab culvert at the head of two channels. One leads eastwards and immediately joins leat 2, the other heads north towards the Old Mill. It starts as a surface channel, leat 5, but further on it is carried on a stone embankment which soon disappears beneath a waste tip. Further on lie the remains of eleven slab pillars, some still bearing wooden stumps of the A-frames which supported the launder to the Old Mill.

A later route for this aqueduct followed a different course. Starting from the original outflow below the dam, leat 5, it curved slightly to the left of and at a higher level than the earlier channel. It skirts around the tip which engulfed the original course by a neatly made slab-walled channel with a sluice, leading to a culvert beneath one of the 15C tips. Within the culvert the original timber channel can be seen. It is 2 feet 6 inches (760 mm) wide between the side pieces, which are 9½ inches (241 mm) high. The aqueduct emerges from the culvert to become a surface leat reinforced with slab sides, and continues on an embankment roughly parallel to the earlier row of pillars. On the embankment the aqueduct consists of a timber flume with planks 2½ inches (63 mm) thick supported at intervals by cross-bearers. The wood is too decayed to measure the width accurately, in fact the roots of young conifers are flourishing in it, but it is similar to that in the culvert.

Further on, the embankment is built of sawn slabs and there is a gap where the aqueduct passed over a tip tramway. The gap was bridged by an extraordinary wooden cistern 31 feet 6 inches (9.6 m) long and 4 feet 2 inches (1.27m) square inside cross section. The sides were of planks set edge to edge and held fast by steel rods, actually long bolts, in holes drilled within the thickness of the planks. The floor was of sheet iron. We found a screen consisting of ⅜ inch (10 mm) diameter rods pitched at 18 per foot run (59 per m) but its precise location in the aqueduct is uncertain. It was too wide to fit between the sides of the cistern, so it was probably placed at its inlet end.

An iron pipe carried the water from the cistern down a sloping ramp to the turbines in the Old Mill. It is likely that the cistern acted as a settling chamber to prevent stones, driftwood etc., from entering the pipe and damaging the turbines. It formed a very prominent landmark in the quarry before it collapsed.

A short distance upstream from the cistern there was a sluice controlling the flow into a branch of the aqueduct which supplied the Lower Mill. It started as a steeply inclined wooden trough 2 feet 6 inches (760 mm) wide and led into a surface channel, leat 6. This leat contoured along the hillside past the Old Mill and the small magazine, ending at a sluice behind and above the Lower Mill. There is supposed to have been a small reservoir or forebay behind the sluice, but although we found traces of a slab-lined enclosure, most of the site has been disturbed by forestry operations and it is impossible to determine the whole of the original ground plan.

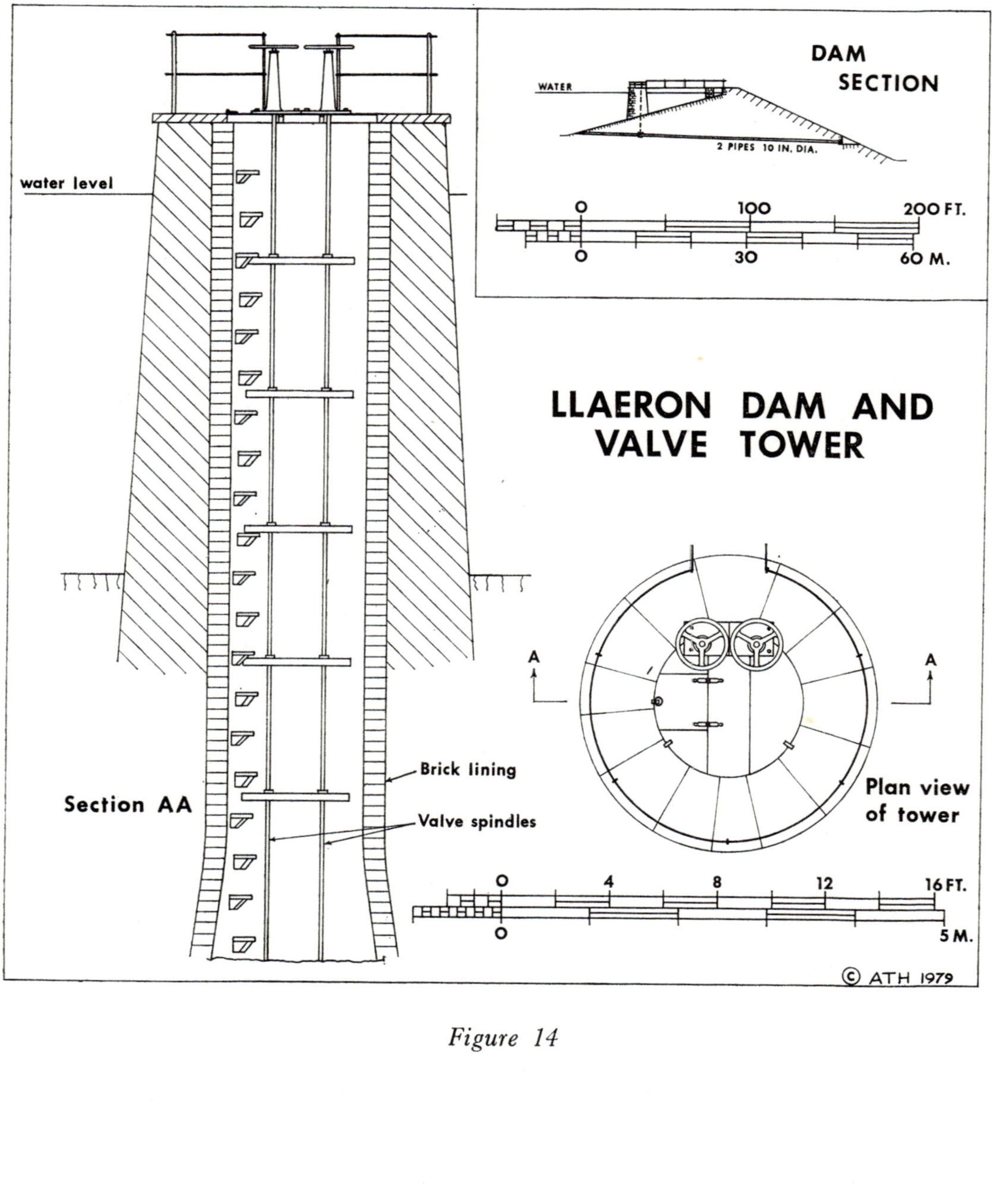
DAM SECTION
WATER
2 PIPES 10 IN. DIA.
0
100
200 FT.
0
30
60 M.
LLAERON DAM AND VALVE TOWER
water level
A
A
Brick lining
Section AA
Valve spindles
Plan view of tower
0
4
8
12
16 FT.
0
5 M.
© ATH 1979

Figure 14

In order to make better use of the Llaeron a new leat (7) was made to connect it to the Boundary Reservoir. It diverged from leat 1 about 775 feet (236 m) from the Llaeron and followed a less steep course so that it could reach the reservoir just inside the dam. It had to cross the spillway by a timber aqueduct, the leat itself having a wooden planked base and sides of slate slab set on edge at each end of the aqueduct.

Llaeron Reservoir

To control the flow of the Llaeron, the Aberdovey Slate Co. built a large reservoir in 1865-6. The works are on an impressive scale, in a different class to the Boundary pond, the capacity being about 15 million gallons (67.5 m litres). The dam consists of soil with a stone facing, see figure 14. On the water side the slope is 15 degrees and the upper 29 feet (8.84 m) is paved with slabs 15 inches (380 mm) deep and the lower end is surfaced with random rubble I foot (300 mm) deep. The top of the dam is capped with a slab wall 10 feet (3 m) wide, and the air side of the dam slopes at 25 degrees. The greatest length measured down the slope on the air side is 101 feet (31 m), and there are overflow channels at each end. At the west end a mortared slab wall backed by earth fill, set at right angles to the dam, forms one side of the channel. The other side is of earth, but both are faced with slabs on edge for the first 33 feet (10 m) and the floor is paved with slabs to form a cascade like a flight of steps. At the outer end of the channel a wide irregular gully runs down to the river. At the other end of the dam the overflow is of slab-faced earth walls and it joins the spillway a short distance from the dam. The surface area of the water was 3.04 acres (1.23 ha).

The Llaeron runs into the reservoir just below a small waterfall near Pont Llaeron. Above the waterfall there is a sluice gate which prevented water entering the reservoir when closed, and the spillway diverges from the river just above the sluice. It has been cut through a large outcrop of rock, involving considerable excavation as witnessed by the tip lying nearby. Further on, the spillway is formed of a slab lined gully which picks up the overflow from the reservoir and leads it down to the river bed. There is another spillway at a lower level whose intake would have been below the waterfall, and it was probably used during construction of the dam before the permanent channel had been excavated.

To the west of the dam there are at least three surface channels above the reservoir, probably used to divert surface water, although no trace of any sluice could be found associated with a small stream running into the reservoir on that side. Spoil for the dam came from an excavation in the hillside on the west side of the reservoir.

The two discharge valves were controlled by handwheels mounted atop a tower built on the water side of the dam. The tower stands some 17 feet (5.2 m) above ground, it is 12 feet 6 inches (3.81 m) diameter at the base and is built of large slabs whose outer faces are dressed to give a smooth conical surface to the exterior. It is lined with engineering bricks and the valve spindles are supported by guides mounted on wooden cross-beams set into the brickwork at 5 feet (1.52 m) intervals. At the top there are two cast iron pedestals surmounted by the handwheels and a sheet-iron platform containing a flap door to give access to the interior. Cast iron steps are fixed to the brickwork. A capping of slate slabs surrounds the iron platform. There was an iron railing around the top and along the catwalk from the dam. It now hangs drunkenly from the top, providing a precarious handhold to those nimble enough to scramble up. There is one slab pier which gave additional support for the catwalk between the dam and the tower.

The intake pipes are 32 feet (9.8 m) long and the outlet pipes discharged onto a slab platform below the dam. One valve retains its spindle and is still operable. The water was apparently released straight into the river subsequently drawn into leat 1. No sluice is visible because of the soil dumped when the dam was breached. The pipes beneath the dam are 10 inches (254 mm) diameter belled out to 1 foot 9 inches (534 mm) at the outlet. Apart from feeding leat 1, water from the reservoir was led via the Llaeron to the pumping wheel near chamber 9B, and in the 1920s sluices were built to supply the wheels on the 8B haulage system and on the Broad Vein.

The waterwheel above 7B was fed by leat 8, connected to leat 3, running into a small forebay some 60 feet (18.3 m) long. Some slabs laid on edge remain at one end and there is a bypass channel running down to the Llaeron. The waterwheel was fed by an overhead launder but nothing remains of it except the base of one slab pillar.

When the main haulage wheels were abandoned, leat 2 continued in use as the diversion channel for the Boundary Stream, but it was perilously close to the edge of the vein. A new channel, leat 9, was cut further back to avoid the risk of subsidence into the open chambers. The sluice for the 8B haulage system was built just above the tramway bridge. A neat slab flume laid on the ground passed beneath the tramway and continued along the top of an old waste tip. At the outer end of the tip the water flowed into a wooden cistern and then into two sheet iron pipes 16 inches (406 mm) diameter. The pipes were supported on a series of slab pillars and from the 8th pillar onwards there was a wooden head-race flume. On the Broad Vein another sluice fed a short aqueduct, probably of timber, to the wheel by B5 adit.

A few years after the quarry closed, fears for the safety of the village caused both reservoirs to be drained and the dams breached. The Llaeron now flows through the gap in the dam, and along its original course as far as the Narrow Vein, where most of it falls into chamber 9B. The Boundary Stream likewise flows into the workings at 1C and eventually the combined waters emerge from the Long Tunnel and pass down the valley to Nant Gwernol.

More power was once extracted from the Gwernol, a small hydro plant lighting the village houses before the National Grid arrived, whilst the writing slate works and a sawmill were both driven by waterwheels in Abergynolwyn.

5

Transport Systems

WE cannot say for certain when tramways were first used at the quarry. The earliest reference we have found is by Robert Williams who wrote that the inventory which he prepared on his arrival in 1862 included 'iron rails'. This probably meant tracks laid in John Pughe's time from the quarry face to the mill via the Daylight Adit. There is no evidence of an exit tramway from the quarry before the advent of the Aberdovey Slate Co. in 1864.

To reach the port of Aberdyfi in the days before the exit tramway, there were two possible routes. One lay over the ridge of Moel-y-Geifr and needed pack animals, whilst the other lay by road down to Tywyn and along the coast road.

Pack horse route

Evidence that pack animals were used is slight, but it was certainly John Pughe's intention in 1847 to carry the slates to the Dyfi wharves by this means. As the quarry became inactive by the late 1850s however, it would have used the route for only ten or twelve years at the most and the path would now be difficult to trace unless it was used by other traffic. In fact the quarrymen who lived in Pennal and lodged at the barracks during the week would have walked over the same path, a practice which lasted at least two generations. There is a footpath shown on the OS plans, and we can only infer that this is the most likely route used by Pughe's pack horses.

From the Old Mill a route to the top of the ridge giving a reasonably even gradient would have been sought. According to the OS first edition plan, there was a footbridge over the diverted Boundary Stream (leat 2) near the reservoir. The path led direct from the Old Mill before the tips were deposited. It runs southwards from the bridge and its course as it climbs the east flank of the spur of Moel-y-Geifr can be followed easily today. It reaches the summit of the ridge at 1,435 feet (438 m) above sea level, the average gradient being 1 in 6.6 (15%).

From the ridge the path runs SSW a short distance along the saddle of Mynydd Rhyd-Galed, after which it turns southwards and crosses a new road. It continues as a well-marked path, through a gate and along the plateau of Mynydd Cefn-Caer. Then it turns SSE to meet a road, grass at first, passing Esgair-isaf Farm and becoming a metalled road which crosses the River Alice, continuing into Pennal village. On the main road there is a gate on the left hand side just outside the village and a footpath which leads to the River Dyfi. Alternatively, a slightly shorter route by-passing the village can be followed. A short distance beyond the Alice bridge, there is a path through a gate on the left which leads past a derelict mill and across the Pandy stream. It then follows the course of the Cwm Ebol tramway and leads to a gate on the A493 almost opposite the footpath leading to the river.

The Dyfi frequently floods over the plain between Machynlleth and the sea, and there is a substantial dyke parallel to the river near Pennal. From the bend in the river at Llyn Draenog to the Cambrian Railway bridge there are extensive traces of wharves along the north bank. At the bend, timber posts with bolt holes near the top ends form the outline of a wharf, with stone rubble lying amongst them. They appear to be relatively recent, and the Thruston Estate is known to have had a wharf at Draenog in the 1890s, charging the public for its use.[1] There are remains of more staging, little more than stumps in the mud, further downstream. It is possible that John Pughe used one or other of these wharves to load slates from his pack horses into light vessels, smacks or dandies, which in turn transhipped their cargoes to sea-going craft at Aberdyfi. Such traffic certainly sailed between Aberdyfi and Derwenlas at that time, carrying slate from the Corris quarries and lead ore from the mines south of the river.

A different route from the quarry to the top of the ridge has been suggested by one writer, involving Pont Llaeron and claiming that John Pughe built this 'pack horse bridge'.[2] This route follows in part the old mountain road from Abergynolwyn up the Gwernol Valley and over the ridge to Pennal and Dyfi Bridge. From Pont Llaeron upwards the road follows a zig-zag course, elaborately banked and ditched, to provide an evenly graded track to the summit. But there seems no point in choosing this route when starting from the quarry since it is much longer and steeper, and involves two crossings of the Llaeron. Pont Llaeron has a carriageway 5 feet 6 inches (1.68 m) wide, much wider than a normal pack horse bridge. The road was probably used by horse drawn sledges having runners at one end and one pair of wheels at the other, a type of vehicle commonly used on Welsh hill farms in the 18th and 19th centuries. Bridges similar to Pont Llaeron exist elsewhere, for example Pont Scethin on

[1] DRO Z/D/AD/92, Thruston Estate Papers.
[2] Mark Bourne, 'Vanishing Welsh Trackways', *Country Life,* 16 September, 1976.

the Harlech-Dolgellau mountain road. It is recorded that Pont Llaeron was in need of repair in 1754.[3]

The length of the pack horse route is $4\frac{1}{2}$ miles (7 km) with a climb of 650 feet (200 m) against the loaded animals. Assuming that each one carried one hundredweight (50 kg) of slates and performed two round trips per day, their capacity would have been around 30 tons each per annum.

Road outlet via Tywyn

As the quarry output increased it became more economical to cart the slates along the turnpike road from Abergynolwyn to Tywyn and Aberdyfi. Robert Williams recalled that they were taken down to Abergynolwyn on sledges (pedrolfenni) each under the control of a driver who hauled the empty vehicle up after each descent. This method was used in many quarries and must have been a hair-raising sight since the road combines the sharpest bends with the steepest gradients! The original route from the Old Mill consisted of a path past Bryneglwys Cottages, crossing the Llaeron by a ford. From Abergynolwyn onwards the road is easy and the total distance from the quarry to Aberdyfi is 11 miles (17.7 km). Another quarry which would have used the same road outlet was Hendre, situated high above Bryneglwys on Tarren Hendre. A plan dated 1855 shows a tramway from the quarry down to the road just west of Abergynolwyn, where slates would have been transhipped into carts.[4] The tramway was never built.

It is likely that horses were changed at Tywyn so that they would not have to work the whole distance under load. An average cartload would probably be ten times the load on a pack horse and this advantage would more than outweight the extra mileage. The condition of the roads however was poor and complaints were often made in the press, as for instance in the *Merionethshire Herald* for 14 November 1863:

> Our roads are in a horrible state, partly owing to the state of the weather; partly owing to the increased heavy traffic, by the cartage of slates from Bryneglwys Quarry . . . but especially owing to the road surveyor's great neglect of repairs.

Local readers of the same journal would have been cheered by the news on 5 December following, namely that Mr. Edward Morgan, Solicitor, informed the meeting of the Ynysmaengwyn Rent Audit of 'an intention to make a railway from Towyn to Bryneglwys, and put steam power upon it.' This is the earliest reference to the Talyllyn Railway known to the writer.

Exit tramway

Although the line from Abergynolwyn to Nant Gwernol is now part of the Talyllyn Railway, it was not so when the quarry was working. The exit tramway extended from the quarry to the former boundary of the Railway Company a

[3] Merionethshire Quarter Sessions Rolls, Calendar, vol. 1, p. 129.
[4] NLW Machynlleth Deeds, Box 1.

short distance east of Abergynolwyn Station. Although part of this line was used by internal traffic, the quarry terminus is conveniently defined as the point just in front of the Old Mill where it crosses the line from the Daylight Adit, since finished slates started their journey to market from there. The tramway ran past the Manager's house in a shallow cutting and crossed the Llaeron by a bridge of 11 feet 6 inches (3.5 m) span, which had substantial abutments of slab. The original I-section beams have almost disappeared due to corrosion, and have been replaced or supplemented over the years by a motley collection of three I-section beams, two timbers and two TR rails. The present deck is of standard gauge sleepers.

The line curved through 90 degrees to the left and ran along a ledge in the hillside, past the Broad Vein workings to the head of Beudynewydd Incline at 24.2 chains (488 m). There was a small weigh-house near the drumhouse, though the weighbridge was apparently on a tip tramway and not the main line. The incline is 710 feet (216 m) long on an average gradient of 1 in 4.9 (20%). At the bottom of the incline the tramway crossed the Llaeron and is then joined by a branch from the Long Tunnel.

This circuitous route raises the question of why the tramway was not laid in a more direct line from the Old Mill. A single incline in place of Beudynewydd and Cantrybedd would have resulted in a shorter, more economical system. The answer may lie in the siting of the mills and the Long Tunnel. All blocks cut from chambers below Adit Level on the Narrow Vein had to be hoisted expensively up to the Old Mill, and it must have been obvious that effort could be saved if they were taken out through the Long Tunnel to a mill built on that level. This possibility was foreseen since the level between the two inclines coincides with the Long Tunnel and a tramway connection was made even before the building of the Lower Mill in 1881. Before then, the Broad Vein workings had to be connected to the Old Mill and the exit tramway served this purpose, although it did hamper their development because it crossed the Vein and prevented the rock beneath from being quarried. Thus the need to have tramway access to the Long Tunnel and a connection from the Broad Vein to the Old Mill led to the route actually chosen for the exit tramway.

The tramway crossed the levelled ground of slate waste in front of the Lower Mill until at Cantrybedd Cottages it reached Cantrybedd Incline and entered the Gwernol gorge. The incline was 440 feet (134 m) long on an average gradient of 1 in 2.75 (36%), and lay partly in cutting near the bottom before emerging to cross the Moelfre stream. A path for horses and pedestrians lay alongside the incline on the west side.

The tramway continued on a narrow ledge on the west flank of the Gwernol gorge, with two passing loops before reaching Alltwyllt (Wild Hill) Incline. This was as far as horses worked the traffic, and there was a small stable at this point. The drumhouse, still *in situ* and being prepared for public display, lies on a ledge above the tramway. This position was necessary because of the change in direction of the line as it reached the incline and ran down the slope instead of along it.

The incline was constructed in three sections. The upper 100 feet is laid on a slab wall at a gradient of 1 in 2.4; the central portion is set upon solid rock, the gradient easing slightly to 1 in 3 for 121 feet. The remainder is again laid on slabs on a gradient of 1 in 4.6. The length overall is 633 feet (193 m) and the average gradient is 1 in 3.53 (28.3%).

The tramway at the foot of Alltwyllt fanned out into three tracks where a rake of loaded wagons could be left to await collection by the locomotive, and empties stored for return to the quarry. It was built partly on a ledge cut from the hillside, partly on slab embankment, but the site of this marshalling yard has been extensively altered to accomodate Nant Gwernol station. The old tramway left the yard on a sharp left hand curve and continued again on a narrow ledge as far as the Village Incline. For much of this distance the track was supported on drystone embankment in a delightful setting amongst trees overlooking the village. Beyond the incline head the line continued to the point where it reached the statutory railway, the Talyllyn Railway, just east of Abergynolwyn station. There was a locomotive watering point by the waterfall at Tydŵr, a simple affair consisting of a wooden flume supported on slab piers, the water being guided into the loco filler by a movable wooden trough. There was also a wooden loco shed at this point. The whole course of the tramway between Abergynolwyn and Nant Gwernol has been regraded and realigned by the TR Company to bring it into line with the requirements of the Department of Environment for a passenger carrying railway.

The branch to the village left the main tramway at 'Abergynolwyn Top Yard' by a double track incline laid upon a drystone embankment, and crossed the Gwernol stream by a girder bridge near the incline foot. The track singled and a turntable gave access to lines serving the writing slate works and a goods shed. Another siding extended along the rear of the houses on the north side of Tan-y-Bryn Street. This siding ran from a loop in the main tramway, which was partly enclosed in a walled compound, the tracks being gated for security. The tramway crossed the main road and passed between the backs of the houses in Llanegryn Street and Water Street. The incline was 363 feet (111 m) long on an average gradient of 1 in 2.58 (39%), the steepest on the line.

Exactly when slate began to flow along the exit tramway is not known, nor has the opening date of the Talyllyn Railway been recorded. The earliest known press report which indicates that slate traffic was running on the TR is dated May 1865, though it may not have been open throughout its length at that date. It is conceivable that slates were brought down the exit tramway to Abergynolwyn village and there transhipped into carts for a short period before completion of the TR, but this is speculation.

Within the span of three years Abergynolwyn had not only become an industrial village, but thanks to the railway it was within a few hours journey time of Birmingham, Liverpool and London. The opening of the railway in Central Wales between 1855 and 1865 brought a profound change to the transport pattern, since before then the speed of travel was limited to that of horse and sail. Robert Williams relates how he and John Lloyd Jones left Llanllyfni

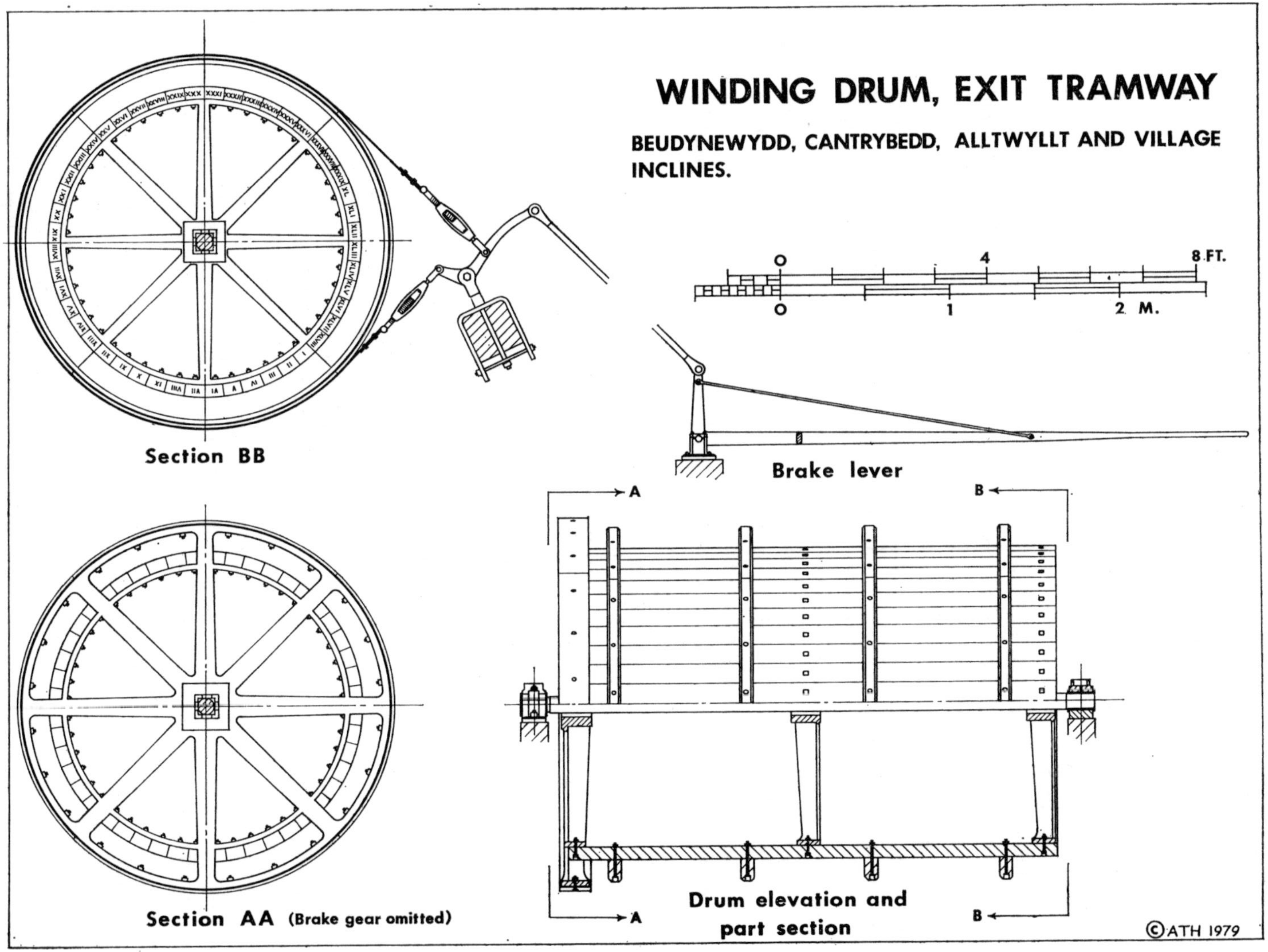
WINDING DRUM, EXIT TRAMWAY
BEUDYNEWYDD, CANTRYBEDD, ALLTWYLLT AND VILLAGE INCLINES.
0
4
8 FT.
0
1
2 M.
Section BB
Brake lever
Section AA (Brake gear omitted)
A
B
Drum elevation and part section
©ATH 1979

Figure 15

The Cantrybedd Incline drumhouse in the early 1950s, with Cantrybedd Cottages on the extreme right.

(J. Adams)

The derelict winding drum at the Village Incline after the drumhouse was demolished.
(Author)

in Caernarvonshire at 5.30 a.m. one day in 1862 and arrived at Talyllyn in the evening, a journey of 58 miles (93 km), having travelled all day in their horse drawn coach. A similar journey by rail a few years later could be accomplished in under 5 hours. The exit tramway enabled slate to be carried down from the quarry economically, but it was vital in other ways also. All materials such as timber, lime and sand for building; quarry equipment, mill machinery and components; coal, oil and domestic provisions, beer for the Railway Inn; all these and more besides could be brought to the quarry and to the doors of the Abergynolwyn houses with ease.

Exit tramway drumhouses

Each of the four drumhouses was individually designed to suit the site conditions, although all the drums and brakes were identical. At Cantrybedd the drum straddled the tramway, but at Beudynewydd the line curved sharply at the summit and did not pass beneath the drum. The Village incline drumhouse was unusual since the main tramway passed through openings in the walls beneath the drum bearings and crossed the incline track on the level. A siding looped off the main tramway and passed behind the drumhouse, a turntable giving access to the incline track. The Alltwyllt drum is set on a rock shelf about 20 feet above the track and is scarcely visible from the tramway except from the incline itself.

Each drum had a timber surface built up from forty-eight planks individually fitted and numbered, bolted to three cast iron spoked disks, see figure 15. It was divided by four wooden collars into two sections each capable of holding thirty-four turns of cable, equivalent to 640 feet (195 m). The shaft was of square cross section, held in each disk by iron wedges which allowed the drum to be centered accurately on the shaft. Each wedge was stamped with an identifying mark so that it could be replaced in the correct position, allowing the drum to be dismantled and transported in pieces for re-assembly on site. The bearings were of simple split pedestal type, bolted to timber bearers set into the drumhouse walls.

An additional rim was provided at one end of the drum, supported on extensions of the spokes, for the brake. An iron ring built up of eight segments was bolted to the periphery, with an insulating sandwich of wood in between. The segmental construction allowed expansion that occurred as it became heated by friction with the brake band, which was of 7 inches × $\frac{3}{8}$ inch (178 mm × 9.5 mm) cross-section. At each end of the band turnbuckles allowed the tension to be adjusted and they were in turn attached to a crank suppored on a timber beam, typically of 11 inches (280 mm) square cross section.

The longer arm of the crank was connected to the brake lever by means of a rod varying in length from 24 feet 5 inches (7.44 m) at the Village Incline to 40 feet (12.3 m) at Alltwyllt. The handlever was over 10 feet (3.2 m) long and gave a leverage of about 7 to 1. It was supported on a double pedestal bearing mounted either on a stout wooden post driven into the ground or on a convenient

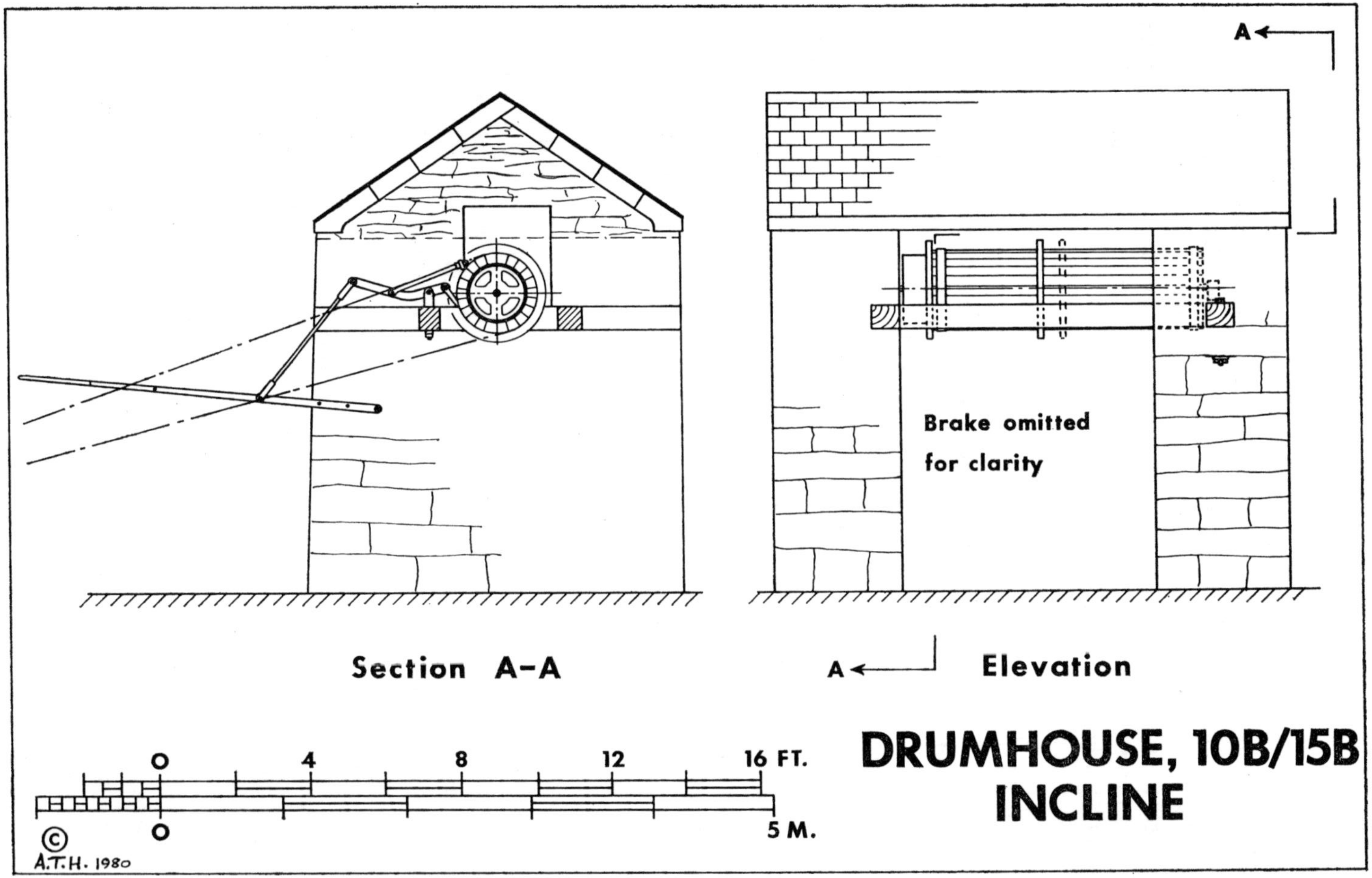
A
Section A–A
A
Elevation
Brake omitted
for clarity
0
4
8
12
16 FT.
0
5 M.
©
A.T.H. 1980
DRUMHOUSE, 10B/15B
INCLINE

Figure 16

piece of rock. The lever was positioned so that the brakeman had a clear view down the incline, but he had no shelter of any kind from the elements.

The inclines operated on the conventional balance system in which the greater weight of the loaded wagons descending under gravity drew up an equal number of empties. Speed was controlled by the brakeman. Occasionally a runaway occured, with spectacular results. In November 1911 the Agent, Meyrick Roberts, was riding up on the last of three wagons on Alltwyllt (an act strictly forbidden by Company rules) and on reaching the top:

> . . . the coupling snapped. Mr. Roberts, with great presence of mind, immediately realised the situation and jumped free of the truck, which made a headlong descent. Failing to negotiate the turn at the bottom of the incline, the truck left the rails and, taking a mighty leap over the river and breaking down a large tree in its flight, landed in a field on the other side, broken into pieces.[5]

The remains of several wagons, victims of similar mishaps, usually caused by cable breakage, lie in the bed of the Gwernol.

Mr. Lewis Roberts recalls his work on the tramway between the wars:

> I was on the slates, loading trucks, I was an incline operator they called it, taking the slates down to meet the train. We loaded six or perhaps eight wagons — two of us working together — you needed the horse just to start them moving but once they were going the gradient was enough to keep them moving. The worst thing the horse was doing was taking the empties back again. There were three inclines and we sent the wagons down two by two — two loaded ones going down, two empties coming up. Sometimes there would be coal coming up and the horse would have to haul it up the gradient above the incline.

Internal tramways

There was an extensive system of tracks in the quarry, above and below ground, and it was altered from time to time to adapt it to the changing needs of the quarry traffic. On each underground floor there were tracks laid from the permanent adit tramways into the working chambers. Wagons loaded with slabs would be run out of each adit, negotiating the inclines or hoists en route to the mills. Wagons full of rubbish (waste rock) were pushed by hand to the nearest tip, the rails being extended as each tip grew, and mill waste was similarly taken from the sheds to the tips. Other lines gave access to the magazine, repair shops, smithy etc., as required.

The Narrow Vein floors were served by conventional balance inclines above Adit Level. There were two on Bryneglwys, 5B/10B and 10B/15B, though the first was probably little used and only the lower parts of the drumhouse walls remains. The 10B/15B drumhouse was virtually intact when we surveyed it, see figure 16, and its construction was typical of the smaller type used in the quarry. The walls are of large dressed, unmortared slabs with openings for access to the drum bearings. The drum is longer than the space between the walls, so a recess

[5] *Cambrian News,* 24 November 1911.

has been formed in one wall to accomodate it. This fact, together with the different coloured slabs in the upper part of the walls, shows that it was rebuilt at some time and the present drum is not the original one. The roof is relatively recent, and the verges are finished with slates neatly trimmed at the eaves, giving a smart appearance. The drum bearings, of unsplit pedestal type, are fixed to a wooden cradle which is built into the masonry. The drum consists of a steel tube clad with wooden planks retained by steel hoops at each end. Spacing collars of timber were simply nailed on, and the brake drum is a shrunk-on iron hoop. The handbrake was applied by a linkage supported on the same cradle as the drum bearings and was actuated by a handle giving a three to one leverage.

The remains of a similar drumhouse were found above the Cwmcwm Incline, though the drum was mounted lower as the track did not pass beneath it. Nothing remains of the drumhouses but the lower walls on the other surface inclines in the quarry.

The 10B/15B incline, which is typical, is laid in a shallow cutting at the bottom and on a drystone embankment higher up. It is 248 feet (75.6 m) long and is laid to an average gradient of 1 in 2.56 (39%). Half way up the incline there is a neatly constructed bridge over the mountain road. The horizontal span is 7 feet 9 inches (2.36 m). There are four I-section beams, laid in two pairs each joined across their top flanges by iron plates. Some lengths of bridge rail are placed across the space between the inner I-beams, their ends laid on the bottom flanges. Rectangular slate slabs are laid between the rails, supported on the flanges and covered with rubble fill, the track being laid on top of this. Additional support for the deck comes from four TR rails beneath the bridge rails.

From the incline foot the tramway ran to the Old Mill, picking up branches from floor 15B and chamber 8B. It lay on a slab embankment, crossing the Llaeron by a simple bridge having two 12 inch (305 mm) square timbers laid across the 18 foot (5.5 m) span. There was a central pier built up from two TR rails, and the bridge sported a timber decking and handrails.

There were several weighbridges on the quarry tramway system, but unfortunately none survive although there was one at Wharf station which is at present in store. The platform of the weighbridge consisted of a cast iron plate which a loaded wagon could be run onto. A balance lever below track level was connected to a steelyard inside the weigh-house so that the weight of the loaded wagon could be measured. The tare weight of the wagon was known, and the load was calculated by difference. The weigh-house was typically a slab building with a large window opening [illegible] the weighbridge and a doorway alongside. There was usually a fireplace and the hut was often used as a messroom by the quarrymen at dinner time. They were sited at strategic points on the tramways, and used to check blocks en route for the mills and in some cases the weight of rubbish taken to the tips, labourers sometimes being paid by the ton of rubbish tipped.

Permanent way

Most of the internal tramway was laid in bridge rail spiked to wooden sleepers. The rest was TR rail used in a few places, for example in the Daylight Adit where some lengths remain, their heads completely worn away. We have found no trace of any type of track at Bryneglwys other than these two varieties of rail spiked to wooden sleepers. The choice of the 2 foot 3 inch (686 mm) gauge was probably made because it was already used in the Corris quarries and on the Corris Railway which opened in 1859. Before the standard gauge lines penetrated Mid-Wales there were several schemes for purely local lines such as the Corris, Machynlleth, Aberdovey and Towyn Railway of 1850,[6] although the gauge is not stated on the plans. Possibly the quarry proprietors envisaged the Corris Railway being extended to Aberdyfi and a tramway from Bryneglwys would meet it at the harbour.

The rail used in the quarry was 20 lb/yd (10 kg/m) standard bridge rail attached to wooden sleepers by dog spikes. Some sleepers were simply logs sawn down the centre. On the main tramways the turnouts had conventional crossings and switchblades, but elsewhere a more primitive type was used. In place of the switchblades there were short lengths of bar which could be swung across to guide the wheels onto the branch, and instead of a crossing another bar was pivotted centrally so that it could be rotated to the appropriate position, see figure 17.

The many wagon turntables in the quarry were of a simple type. An iron plate with chequer pattern cast into the top surface had two pieces of 1½ inch (38 mm) square bar bolted on to act as rails, whilst the base had cast-in slots at the periphery to locate the tramway rails. A more substantial pattern was used at the head of the Village Incline on the exit tramway. Neither type bore any maker's mark, although others to a different pattern still at Towyn Wharf are from Thos. Dunn & Co., Manchester.

The track on the exit tramway from the top of Alltwyllt to the TR boundary and on the Village Incline was laid in TR materials. The rails were rolled in wrought iron to a rather squat flat-bottom profile of approximately 40 lb/yd (19.9 kg/m) and each one was 21 feet (6.4 m) long. They were carried on wooden sleepers of 8 inches × 3½ inches (203 mm × 89 mm) section, 5 feet (1.52 m) long. The sleepers were pitched at 3 feet (.91 m) centres, the joints being supported in cast iron chairs without fishplates. The joint chairs were only 5½ inches (140 mm) wide and the rail ends were held by wooden keys, so a high standard of maintenance was required. Narrower chairs were used on two intermediate sleepers, the other four having dog spikes, a somewhat unusual arrangement. Sleepers had to be packed to different levels according to whether they had chairs or spikes. The chairs were attached to the sleepers by round-headed iron pins with plain shanks.

Turnouts had special chairs to two types to support the switchblades, and were controlled by a weighted lever, the weights being enclosed in a cast iron

[6] DRO Qr/r/(xx).

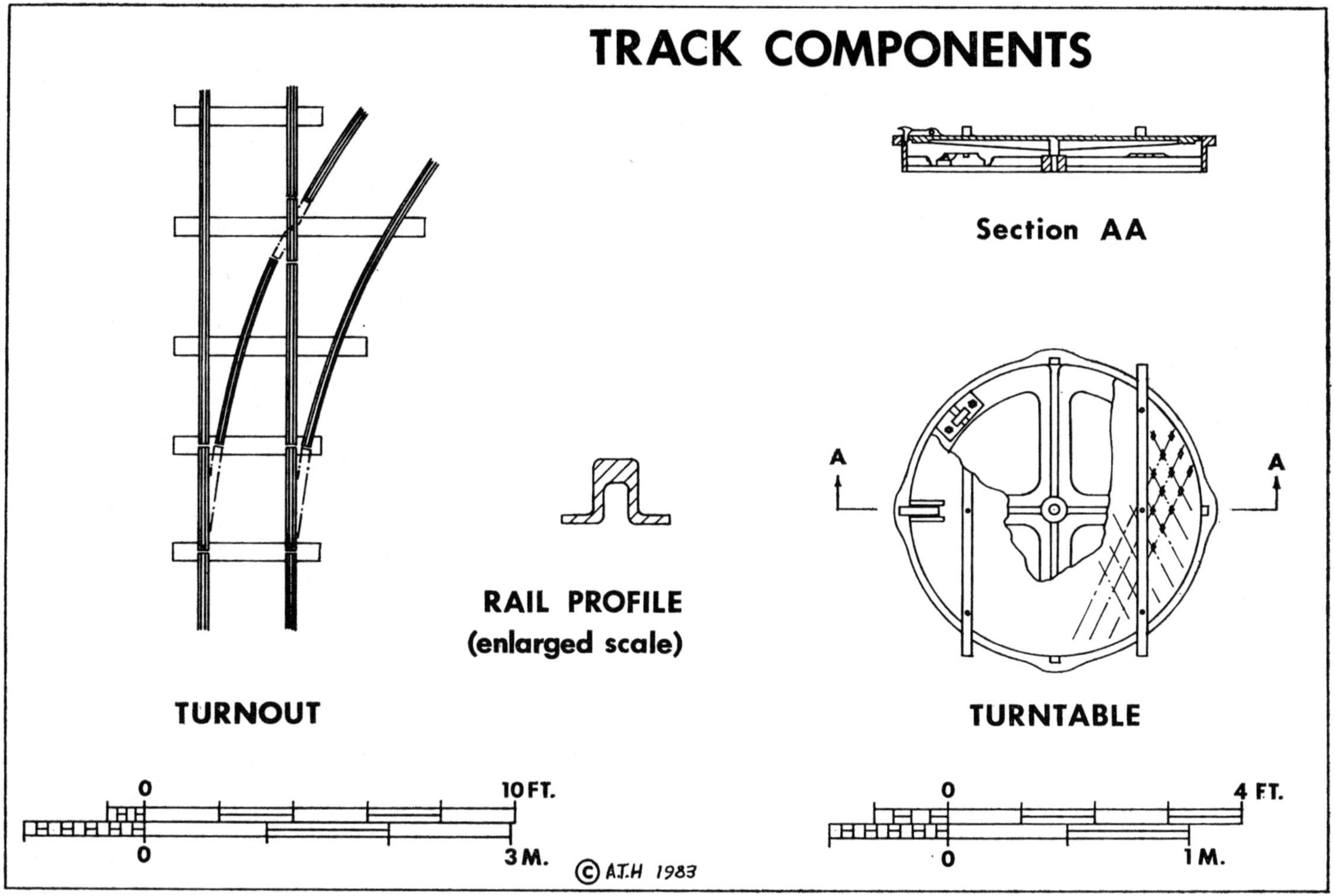
TRACK COMPONENTS
Section AA
A
A
RAIL PROFILE
(enlarged scale)
TURNOUT
TURNTABLE
0
10 FT.
0
3 M.
© A.T.H 1983
0
4 FT.
0
1 M.

Figure 17

box set into the ground. Some turnouts had no levers, the blades being simply kicked into the required position. The cast iron parts of the turnouts bear the mark 'JB & Sons', denoting John Bagnall & Sons which is now a subsidiary of F. H. Lloyd Holdings. A complete example recovered from Abergynolwyn Top Yard is displayed at the Narrow Gauge Railway Museum at Tywyn Wharf.

Wagons

The 'Block and Rubbish' department had 150 or more wagons, two types being reserved for use in the quarry, one for carrying slabs to the mills and the other for waste rock to the tips.. The slab wagon was a neat and economical design with a timber frame, see figure 18. It had four wooden transoms faced with iron strips and an iron drawbar fitted with D-links and coupling hooks. The bearings were simple unmetalled castings, the wheels being free to rotate on the axles, retained by cotter pins. The loose wheels and short wheelbase made these wagons well suited to the sharp curves of the quarry tracks. The same applies to the rubbish wagons, which had shorter but otherwise similar underframes and sheet metal bodies open at one end. The loaded wagon was run onto the tip, eventually being stopped suddenly by the upturned rail ends at the outer end of the tip, which caused the contents to be shot forward out of the wagon. The solebars were cut back at the end so that it could be tipped right up to help discharge the rubbish.

For carrying finished slates and slabs from the quarry down to Wharf, there were two variants of a timber bodied wagon whose design was typical of the period. The underframes were of stout timbers with morticed cross beams, the solebars being extended to form dumb buffers reinforced with iron hoops. The cast iron axleboxes were unsprung and some bore the mark of Isaac, Portmadoc. The wheelbase was 2 feet 8 inches (813 mm), the iron wheels were 1 foot 6 inches (457 mm) diameter and of two types — curved and straight spoked. Bandbrakes acted on the wheels on one side only, operated by a handlever normally supported in the off position by a chain. The wagon had a sheet iron floor and wooden bar type sides and ends, the bars being morticed at the corner joints and supported on cast iron bobbins. One type had two bars, the other had three. A specimen of the two-bar type is displayed at the Narrow Gauge Railway Museum.

The TR possessed iron bodied and timber sided wagons of several types, and some of them would have travelled to the quarry loaded with coal, lime, timber etc. There was also a gunpowder van used to deliver explosives transhipped from the coast line at Wharf station. There were none of the trestle type slab wagons which were popular on the Corris Railway.

The motive power on the internal tramway was man and animal throughout the quarry's existence. This applied to the exit tramway as far as Alltwyllt, the TR locomotives working to the foot of that incline. At the peak of production the average daily output was no more than 30 tons, only a fraction of the railway's capacity, so the equipment had an easy life and survived unchanged

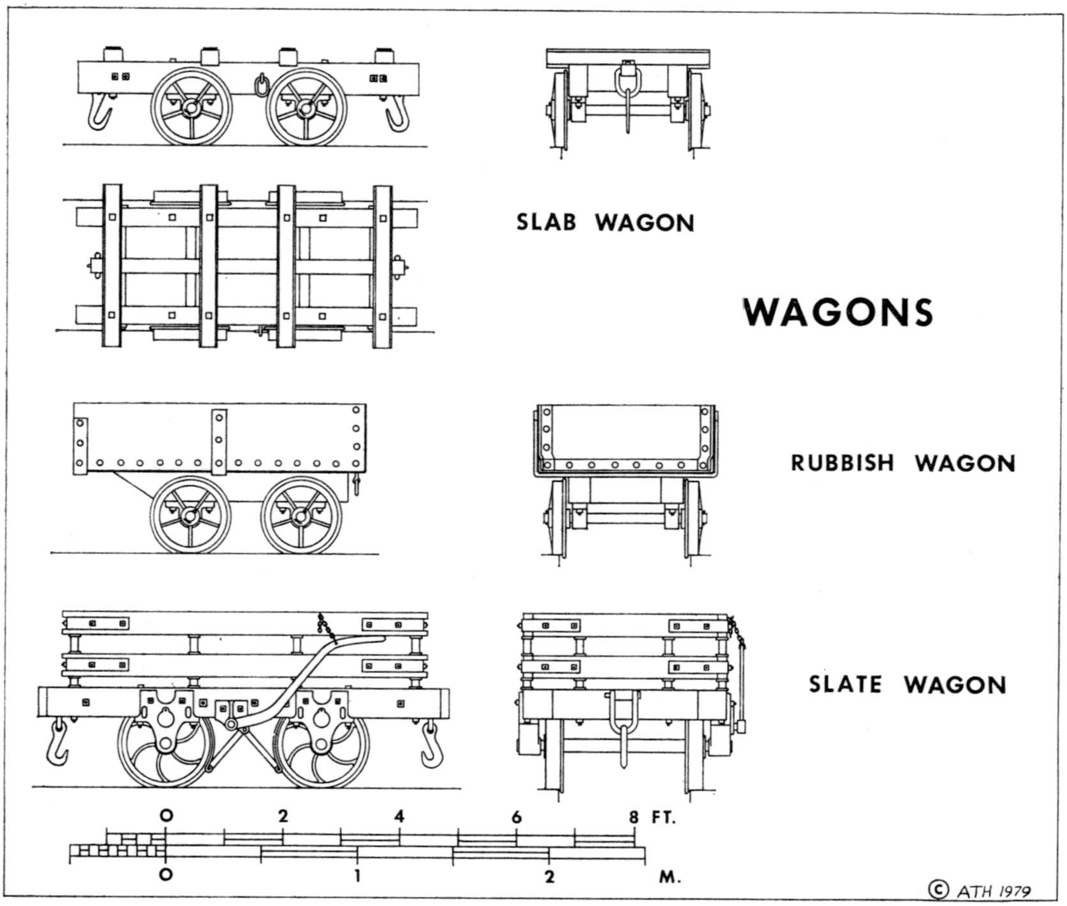
SLAB WAGON
WAGONS
RUBBISH WAGON
SLATE WAGON
0
2
4
6
8 FT.
0
1
2
M.
© ATH 1979

Figure 18

throughout the quarry's existence. It was a case of making do and patching up in later years as rails became worn until they split and sleepers crumbled to dust beneath the turf which alone held the rails to gauge. Slab wagons had such deep grooves worn into their wheels that they looked at first glance like the double-flanged variety. This romantic decrepitude lasted until the quarry closure in 1947, the track between Abergynolwyn Station and the foot of Alltwyllt remaining in place until swpet away by the Nant Gwernol extension works of the Talyllyn Railway. The remainder of the tramway had been lifted except for one or two odd lengths in 1952. Fortunately the Alltwyllt drumhouse survived *in situ* to be saved for preservation.

The Port of Aberdyfi

The opening of the Aberystwyth and Welsh Coast Railway, later part of the Cambrian Railways, did not render the port of Aberdyfi obsolete. In fact the railway brought slate traffic to the wharves from Tywyn and Machynlleth, which originated from the quarries at Bryneglwys and Corris respectively until the demise of the coastal sailing trade about the time of the First World War. The proportion of Bryneglwys output carried in this way between 1884 and 1887 for example was 58%.[7] of 151 such consignments from September 1883 to May 1888, 69 went to Irish destinations and 73 to English ports distributed widely around the south-west, south and east coasts. These cargoes were carried mainly by schooners in loads ranging from 45 to 233 tons, averaging 116 tons. From 1895 the tonnages are not quoted in the register, but assuming the same ratio of cargo weight to registered tonnage as in the earlier period, we can estimate the approximate totals from 1895 until the last shipment in 1915 (See Appendix 3). After 1903 no Irish destinations appear in the record, nearly all consignments going to ports in Southern England, Gloucester and Faversham taking nearly half between them. Except for a brief rally in 1904-06 the picture is one of steady decline until 18 May 1915 when the schooner *Mary Edwards* took the last recorded cargo of Bryneglwys slate, from Aberdovey to Bideford.

The smack 'Seven Brothers'

Although strictly outside the scope of the quarry history, an account of this ship is given because of its general interest as it was owned by the McConnels, and because of the important part played by the coastal traders in the slate business. The registration certificate, dated 15 August 1853 shows that the *Seven Brothers* was built by Rowland Evans at Derwenlas. She was of 43 tons burthen, 48 feet long, 14 feet wide and 8 feet deep in her hold amidships. (14.6 m × 4.27 m × 2.44 m)

> . . . she is smack rigged, with a running bowsprit; is square sterned carvel built; has neither galleries nor figurehead; the Frame work and planking are of wood . . .

[7] DRO Z/M/604/1.

Her ownership was divided into the customary sixty-four shares, fourteen belonging to William Davies, Master Mariner of Tywyn. The other owners consisted of seven shopkeepers, one farmer, one joiner, one spinster and another master mariner, all except one living in Tywyn, Aberdyfi or Machynlleth. It was thus a local enterprise and reflected the boom in trade which occurred in the early 1850s. Apart from the Managing Owner, William Davies, seven other members of the Davies family appear in the crew lists of the 1850s. Judging by their ages it is just possible that they were the 'Seven Brothers' that gave the ship its name, William being their uncle or guardian.[8]

William Davies sailed his ship up and down the shores of Britain plying the coastal trade from Glasgow to Bridgwater in the west, from Falmouth to Shoreham in the south and to Irish ports from Ramelton to Cork. His two-man crew consisted of mate and boy who with very few exceptions were local men from Cardigan Bay, mainly Aberdyfi, Tywyn and Borth. The boys varied in age, the youngest being eleven but were generally between thirteen and twenty-one.

All manner of cargoes were carried besides slates, such as coal, lead ore, limestone, pig iron, bark and timber. The vessel was rarely at sea for more than ten days at a stretch, typical voyages taking four days (Aberdyfi to Cardiff) and five days (Aberdyfi to Dungarvan, near Waterford). In a good year it would cover over 3,000 miles spread over twenty voyages. The pattern of trade changed over the years, most voyages in the 1850s involving English ports whereas from the late 1860s onwards Ireland figures more frequently in the lists. Scottish ports never appear more than twice in any one year. James Morgan, father of D. W. Morgan who wrote the book *Brief Glory* containing a first hand account of the port of Aberdyfi, captained the ship in January 1870. Shortly afterwards T. H. McConnel acquired all the shares in the *Seven Brothers* and after his death the ownership passed to William McConnel. In 1873 William Roberts of Tywyn joined the ship as mate and three years later he became master. On Saturday 21 April 1877 when the ship was homeward bound from Waterford and near the Tuskar Rock, Roberts was knocked overboard by the boom and drowned. He was 31 and according to local reports he left a wife and several children.[9] David Bowen, formerly of the *Maglona* succeeded him as master.

In 1878 notices of an auction to be held on 23 April appeared, the ship having been 'recently thoroughly overhauled and fitted with new sails and all other seagoing requisites'.[10] Despite this recommendation David Davies, the new owner, had to have large repairs carried out including a new deck before Lloyds would class it A1 for a further ten years. He lived at Amity House, Borth, and became owner of his dubious bargain on 4 May 1878. The following year he was reported by the contemporary ancestor of the traffic warden to the Tywyn Local Board, whose clerk was directed to write complaining

[8] PRO Records of the Reg. General of Shipping and Seamen, class BT 98.
[9] *Cambrian News*, 27 April 1877.
[10] *Carnarvon and Denbigh Herald*, 6 April 1878.

> . . . of the manner in which he moors his vessel and informing him that if he did not desist from passing the rope through the wall, and fastening it in such a manner as to endanger the wall and choke the gutter, proceedings would be taken against him.[11]

But after only eight voyages in his freshly repaired vessel she came to grief off the Calf of Man, whilst on passage to Coleraine, on 12 August 1880. The crew were saved and taken to Douglas where they were discharged on the following day.

Little trace remains today to show that ships once sailed up to Derwenlas. The village lies on the southern margin of the valley, which has a wide floor with hills rising steeply on each side. The river meanders across the flood plain and the builders of the Aberystwyh and Welsh Coast Railway diverted it at Derwenlas to avoid the expense of erecting two bridges across it.[12] In order to maintain access to the wharves which would otherwise be cut off, part of the original course of the river was retained and one bridge had therefore to be built, and it still exists.

There were three wharves, reputedly known as Tan-y-ffordd, Quay Ellis and Quay Ward.[13] The furthest upstream of these was Tan-y-ffordd where an old building, possibly a warehouse still stands with its back close to the main road. The wharf site is now a scrapyard and the redundant portion of the river bed has been filled in. This was the furthest point reached by the Corris, Machynlleth and River Dovey Tramroad according to the deposited plans of the Aberystwyth and Welsh Coast Railway, even though the C.M.R.D.T. Act empowered the Company to run as far as Garreg, over two miles (3½ km) downstream.[14]

Quay Ellis lay a couple of hundred yards (200 m) below Tan-y-ffordd, also on the site of the filled-in-leg of the river. At Quay Ward however, the site is still on the water's edge and stonework of the original wharf can be seen just below the surface. Ships were reputedly built at Tan-y-ffordd, Quay Ward and at Llyn Bwtri, and the *Seven Brothers* must have been laid down at one or other of these yards.

When the railway bridge at Dyfi Junction was built it had a section which could be rolled back to allow ships to pass, the cottage on the north bank being provided for the keeper. There is a ruined house called *Maenen* on the south bank just upstream of the bridge. It was a tavern, serving the needs of the crews of sailing vessels using the wharves or on passage between Derwenlas and Aberdyfi. This journey took two tides, the boats pausing at Draenog whilst awaiting the next tide. There are graffiti on the walls of *Maenen* such as 'T. Jones 1856'.

The Cambrian Railways built a new pier at Aberdyfi in 1882 and it survived until long after the demise of traffic.[15] The old warehouses are still there, new

[11] DRO Minute Book of the Towyn Local Board, 12 June 1879.
[12] DRO QR/r (xi).
[13] Powis Land Club, *Montgomeryshire Collection*, Vol. 51, p. 75.
[14] DRO QR/r (xi).
[15] DRO. Plan of Cambrian Railways proposed Pier.

uses having been found for them, and the pier has been replaced with a new one of similar pattern though smaller in size. The memories of Aberdovey the sea-port are fading and a unique way of life, that of the merchant seaman under sail, has disappeared completely.

6

Domestic Buildings and Village

IN the 1840s and 50s when the quarry was being worked on a small scale, Abergynolwyn was only a hamlet and most people in the district, including quarrymen, lived in small groups of cottages or lodged in isolated farmhouses. Today the ruins of many abandoned houses remain in the Gwernol Valley and by the roadside west of the village. When the Aberdovey Slate Company expanded the quarry in the 1860s it built some seventy houses in Abergynolwyn, which became a quarry village overnight. At the quarry they built more houses, including a large one for the manager and barracks for those men living too far afield to commute daily.

Early period (pre-1864)

A cottage typical of the 1840s, but now demolished, stood by the main road opposite Abergynolwyn station drive. It was a terrace of three 'one up and one down' houses each a mere 12 feet 6 inches (3.8 m) wide by 16 feet 6 inches (5 m) deep inside. If the 1861 census returns are to be believed, there were fourteen people including four small children living in those six rooms, which works out to 88 square feet (8.2 m^2) per head. The ground floor room of one house had a wooden partition part way across, forming a small kitchen or scullery at the back, and a step ladder led vertically up to the room above. The walls were of unsawn slab and the roof was of course of slate, and a tablet above the entrance of the middle one bore a carved inscription:

Y TAY YMA
Adeiladwyd gan
JOHN ROBERTS
Perchenog Llwyn-y-fynwent
Yn y flwyddyn 1848

(These houses here were built by John Roberts owner of Llwyn-y-fynwent in the year 1848). The word TAY (houses) is a mis-spelling of TAI. They were known as Bwlch Cyfyng (Narrow Cutting) from the location at the narrowest point of the valley. Llwyn-y-fynwent, named in the inscription, is a ruined house on the opposite side of the valley just below the platform at the west end of the station.

There were at least seven dwellings in the Gwernol Valley prior to the mid-1860s developments, and most were lived in by quarrymen at some time. Nant Llwyn-gwedd and Hendrewallog are believed to date from the sixteenth century. Both are sited down rather than across the slope of the hill, a common practice in old Wales. Hendrewallog was the last to be lived in, becoming deserted in the 1970s.

Nearer to the river lies Beudynewydd (New Cowshed) Farm, now a pair of semi-detached two storey houses. The upstairs rooms lay within the roof space, which was lined with at least seven layers of wallpaper when we surveyed it, and was reached via a vertical step-ladder. A cottage called Beudybach (Small Cowshed) lies buried beneath the Broad Vein tips a short distance up the valley. Bryneglwys Farmhouse was a double-fronted two storey building constructed of stone, and had a stable built on to the south gable end. A hayloft above the stable was reached by an external stone staircase, and there were other buildings nearby including a barn and a more modern cowshed. George Smith, the quarry Agent and his family, probably lived there in 1851.

Bryneglwys Cottages were extensively altered by the Aberdovey Slate Company, but in George Smith's day they formed a single storey block of two or possibly three cottages. There was a substantial wall between rooms 2 and 3 (see figure 19) with fireplaces each side and built into it was a massive timber frame which supported the original roof. The wall between 3 and 4 had a doorway cut through it at each end and it was possibly the original end wall, 5 being added later.

On the hillside amidst the forest above Cantrybedd Cottages a large stone-built farmhouse called Frondeg lies in ruins. It is probably as old as Bryneglwys Farm, and certainly predates the quarry.

The 1851 census returns record sixteen households and three uninhabited houses in the 'hamlet of Abergynolwyn'.[1] They were grouped around Pandy Square. Pandy is a farmhouse, but its name and riverside location show that it is the site of a fulling mill. On both sides of the main road in the village there are several small stone cottages, still inhabited, which pre-date the 1860s developments. Some are single storey, some double, and their uses were not always exclusively domestic. At various times one became a post office, another a smithy and others shops. According to the 1851 census, two heads of household were quarrymen and in the Township of Maestrefnant, which included the Gwernol Valley, six out of fourteen quarrymen were from Llanllyfni, Caernarvonshire.

[1] DRO 1851 Population Census for Merioneth, parish of Llanfihangel-y-Pennant.

Despite this influx of quarrymen, the scattered pattern of the community persisted and no new houses were built to accomodate them. They either lodged with local families or rented existing houses. It was the coming of the Aberdovey Slate Company in 1864 that transformed this rural backwater and created an industrial village almost overnight. The scale of their operations demanded a workforce much larger than could be quartered in the existing houses, and it attracted labour from the adjoining counties of Montgomery and Caernarvon.

Company housing from 1864

For the men who lived too far away for daily commuting the Company built two large barracks at the quarry. They boarded during the week, paying a rent of one shilling (5p) per month in 1894. The Talyllyn ran special trains for them, charging half the ordinary fare, the Up working leaving Tywyn at 6 a.m. on Mondays and a return working leaving Abergynolwyn at 1.30 p.m. on Saturdays. This was altered to run on Fridays at 6.15 p.m. after the five day working week was introduced in 1889.

The main Barracks was a fine building, see figure 19, different in layout to those generally found in the industry. With walls of dressed slab two feet thick, quoin stones having chamfered corners and main windows boasting planed slate sills, it stood out from the plain huts around it. The roof purlins extended beyond the walls and had ogee-carved ends. A single entrance near the right hand end of the front elevation opened into a hallway with a small store or pantry to the rear and a staircase leading up to the landing above. A doorway led into a large dining room lit by eight sash windows, and there was a substantial brick fireplace against the north wall. The effect was rather spoilt by a matchboard partition across the room to form the caretakers accommodation, itself divided into two rooms with fireplaces in each. The main room was further cluttered by a wooden staircase to the right of the fireplace. The walls were plastered and painted inside, the ceiling was of plaster supported by slates nailed to the joists. Each slate had holes to give a 'key' to the plaster.

Upstairs, the sleeping quarters occupied the space directly above the dining room. The dormitory was divided into three sections by matchboard partitions nailed to the roof trusses. The gable on the north side gave an air of spaciousness, and the chimney must have made this a coveted spot on winter nights! Each section was 12 feet (3.66 m) long and there were probably three beds along each outside wall, totalling eighteen altogether. This would give about 225 cubic feet (6.38 m^3) per man. The dining room was certainly shared by the men in the other barracks. At the west end of the dormitory the doorway led to a landing with some built-in cupboards under the eaves, probably for storing bedding materials. There were two small privies behind the main building.

The barracks probably dates from 1865-6 and it appears on the 1871 census returns but as these were gathered on a Sunday the men were away at their homes. There was however a resident family consisting of a mechanic, his wife and daughter and a sixteen year old servant girl. The womenfolk doubtless attended to the cooking and cleaning for the men who lodged there.

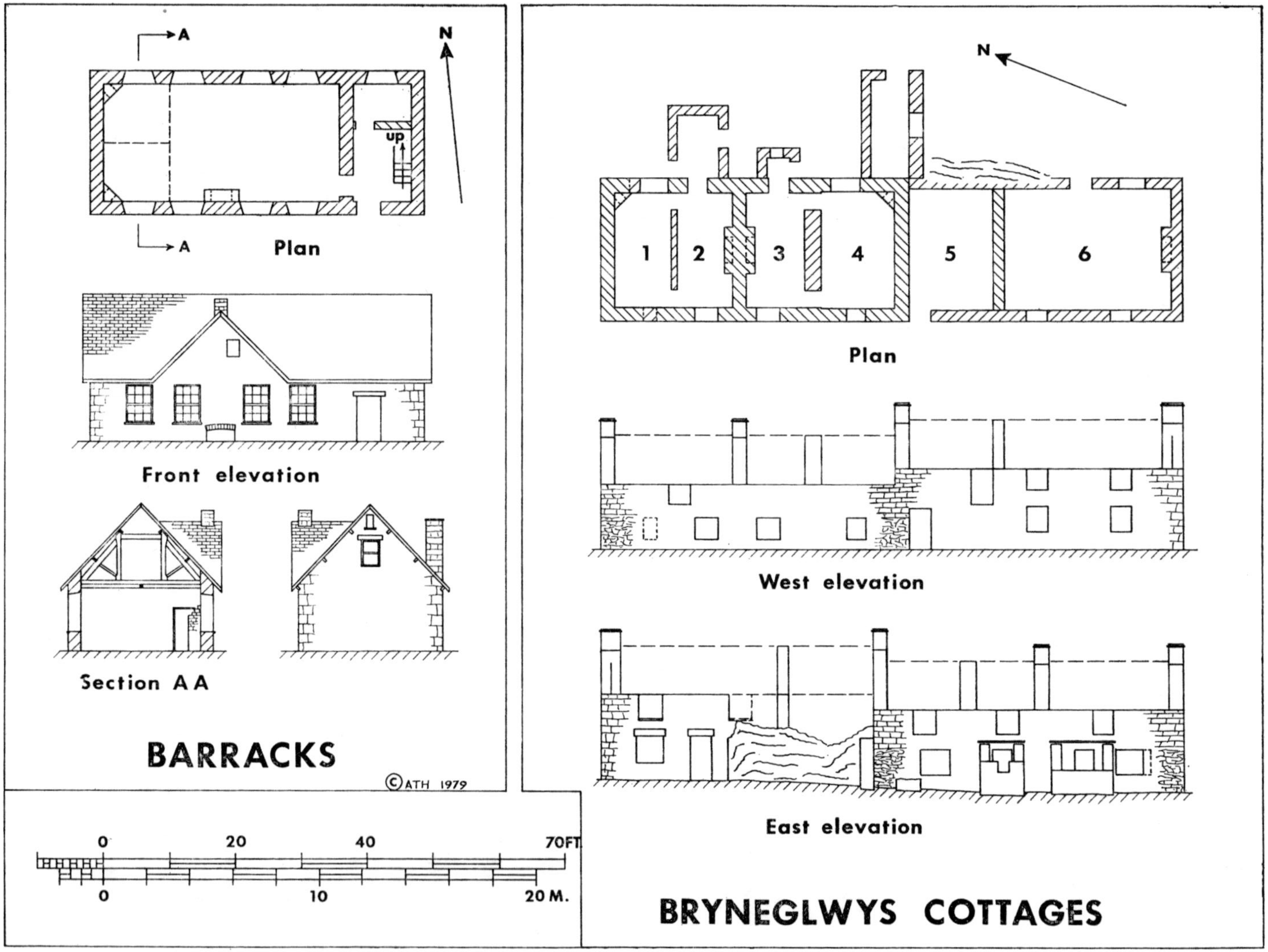
A
N
up
A
Plan
Front elevation
Section AA
BARRACKS
©ATH 1979
0
20
40
70FT
0
10
20 M.
N
1
2
3
4
5
6
Plan
West elevation
East elevation
BRYNEGLWYS COTTAGES

Figure 19

A group photographed in the village. Left to right, Jane Williams, Gwen Parry, Annie Davies, Jane Pugh, Kitty Davies (with child in arms), wife of Rees Pugh, Jane Pugh, Mary Roberts, Mary Jones and Elin Humphries.

(Caradog Jones collection)

The Manager's House, 1985.

(Author)

A vivid description of the Barracks appeared in a local paper in March 1873[2]:

> Snow and hail were the harbingers of the sabbath day, and there being a small Sunday School in the 'barracks' attended by the few who reside in the vicinity of the slate quarry I passed a few hours therein . . . The room was a huge kitchen, filled with the usual culinary utensils. Slung to the rafters were sides of bacon, hams, strings of onions, a lantern, net of soap etc., and during the meeting the saucepan bubbled merrily on the fire . . .

A hundred years later, the hooks which supported the sides of bacon were still there! Clearly it was not just a barracks, but a centre for social activities, Sunday School, concerts and so on. The ground in front still bloomed with primulas, raspberries and other survivors of the gardens tended by the men in their free hours. Not all who lodged in the barracks travelled on the Talyllyn Railway, some walked over the hills from Pennal and even further afield on Monday mornings in time for a 7 a.m. start.

A second barrack was provided over the carpenter's shop. This was built in sawn slab on top of the single storey workshop, see figure 12. There were three large windows in the north wall but none in the south because of the waste tips close behind it. The room was reached by an external slate slab staircase leading to a door at the west end, and there was a fireplace built into the back wall. It was 38 feet 6 inches by 18 feet 3 inches (11.7 m by 5.6 m) inside, somewhat larger than the main barrack and had space for about 24 men. It was probably built by 1870 and is shown on the 1887 O.S. plan.

Still more living space was needed so Bryneglwys Cottages were extended. An upper storey and a new two-storey extension to the south end all in sawn slab converted the cottages into a typical industrial urban terrace — in the middle of a field. Room 6 formed a new double-fronted house, whilst 5 alone had its entrance at the back and lacked a fireplace, so was probably a storeroom. There were several outbuildings, some doubtless being privies, and the two older houses had large lean-to entrance porches added on. In the 1871 census there are eighteen people, including eight children, listed under Bryneglwys Cottages and there were doubtless more lodging during the week.

The tenants of Cantrybedd Cottages were luckier. As if to make amends for the makeshift job on Bryneglwys, their houses were constructed to a much superior standard. Two of the three terraced houses were 11 feet wide by 20 feet 6 inches deep inside (3.4 m by 6.3 m), the third considerably wider at 18 feet (5.5 m). Each house had large sash windows front and rear, a wooden staircase and internal partitions made in the same style as the Barracks ceiling, predating modern plasterboard techniques. A timber studding was built to support the slates which carried the plaster. A doorway was cut through the party wall between the upstairs rooms of 2 and 3 (figure 20), presumably when both were occupied by the same tenant. The outbuildings included a bakery, 4, with a 'beehive' oven and three privies, 7, one being larger than the other

[2] *Carnarvon and Denbigh Herald,* 15 March 1873.

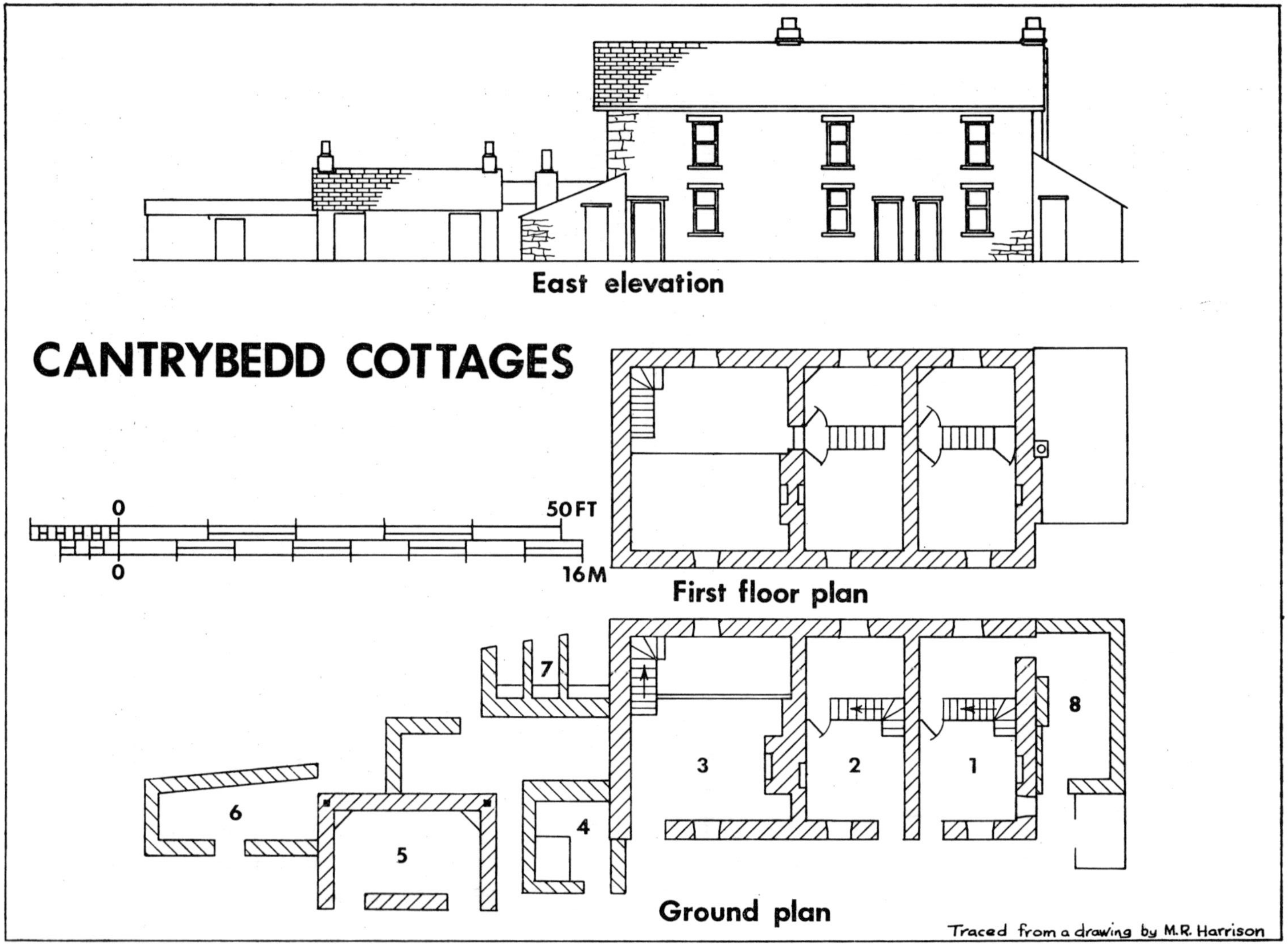

East elevation
CANTRYBEDD COTTAGES
0
50FT
0
16M
First floor plan
7
8
3
2
1
6
4
5
Ground plan
Traced from a drawing by M.R. Harrison

Figure 20

two — a reflection of the house plan! 5 was probably a stable, the fire being used to boil water for mash, and 6 a coal store. We found a large wooden vessel, like one half of a barrel, with a cast iron handle, in room 6. It contained some heavy oil, still partly liquid beneath a mass of soil and vegetation, which was probably used to lubricate the incline ropes. A lean-to extension 8 lay against the smaller end house, with a communicating door cut through. It had a fireplace and a chimney of earthenware drain pipes. Water was drawn from a well behind the houses.

Keeping watch over these scattered tenements, the Manager's House occupied a central position in the valley. Sometimes called Bryneglwys Hall, it was an imposing Victorian villa built in the 1860s. In plan it was L-shaped and was constructed of slab with slates hung vertically on the front elevation against the north winds. An entrance porch protected the front door, which opened onto a central hallway with large rooms each side, see figure 21. Room 2 led to the kitchen 3 and a small room 4. The upstairs plan was similar, each room having a fireplace, 7 and 8 being reached via a small ante-room off the landing. There was no evidence of an internal bathroom or toilet, nor of any plumbing within the main building. A small extension built onto the back of the house was probably a laundry, 5, as it had the remains of a waste pipe and a bowl shaped impression in the masonry, water being heated over the fireplace provided. Within the walled yard, which was roofed over, there were three cubicles with the remains of a w.c. in the centre one. Some piping attached to the wall indicates that water may have been plumbed in from the Llaeron at least for the closet, some piping being found buried in the ground between the house and the stream. In the yard stood a baker's oven like the one at Cantrybedd. A large walled garden contained fruit trees which still produce apples and plums in a good year.

At the back of the Manager's house stood the quarry office. It had two main rooms, 11 and 12, but as there was originally no connecting doorway between them 12 was probably a later addition. This is borne out further by the fact that the fireplace of 11 was built into the wall but that in 12 was added on. The four main windows were large and boasted planed slate sills supported by carved corbels, although the one facing the house had been converted into a doorway. Good views over the quarry area could be had through these windows. The wall dividing 10 and 11 is a curious feature as it formed a very confined space (10) and effectively blocked the window.

A terrace of six cottages is depicted on a drawing dated July 1864 for 'T. H. McConnel Esqr, Bryn Eglwys Slate Quarry' signed by James Stevens, Architect but there is no building corresponding to the plan at Bryneglwys or Abergynolwyn.[3] It may possibly have been intended to replace the single storey Bryneglwys Cottages before the decision was taken to enlarge them by simply adding the upper floor, doubtless on the grounds of cost.

On the night of the 1871 Census there were sixty-three people including two

[3] Plan in possession of P. Roberts, Esq.

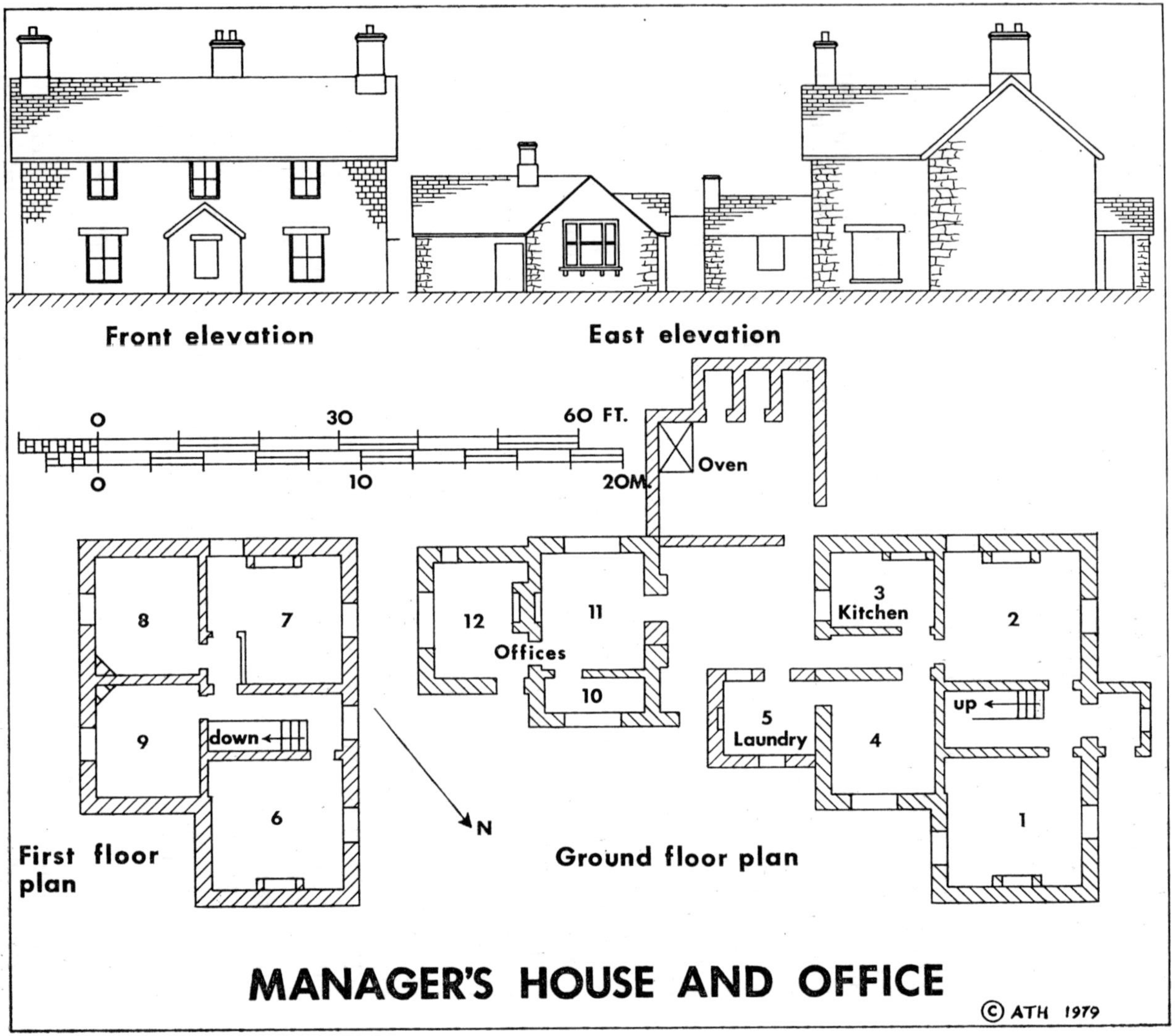
Front elevation
East elevation
0
30
60 FT.
0
10
20M.
Oven
8
7
9
down
6
12
11
Offices
10
3
Kitchen
2
5
Laundry
4
up
1
N
First floor plan
Ground floor plan
MANAGER'S HOUSE AND OFFICE
© ATH 1979

Figure 21

visitors in twelve households in the Gwernol Valley.[4] Twenty-four were aged under eighteen and nineteen were employed at the quarry. On weekdays of course their numbers would be increased by the men lodging in the barracks and houses. Despite this sizeable population in what is now an uninhabited valley, the main centre of domestic and community life was Abergynolwyn village.

Development of Abergynolwyn

Prior to the 1860s the standard of housing locally was primitive and the Corbet Estate Act of 1862 for example recites:

> . . . the present house accommodation (of Aberdovey and Towyn) is wholly inadequate . . . the inhabitants are suffering from the want of proper dwelling houses, and disused stables and dark hovels are fitted up as dwellings for numbers of the poorer classes resident there . . .[5]

The major development of the village took place in the mid-1860s when the Aberdovey Slate Company built seventy-one houses in three main groups. Along Llanegryn Street they erected a row of twenty-four single storey double-fronted houses in two terraces of twelve. Behind these are twenty-four larger houses in three terraces facing the River Gwernol across Water Street. The far end of these streets reaches almost to the group of older houses at the hamlet of Cwrt which lies by the bridge over the Dysynni known as Pont-y-Cwrt (Tannery Bridge). The other Company development was Tan-y-Bryn Street, where numbers 1 to 12 form a terrace of single fronted two-storey houses opposite a terrace of similar length but containing only eleven houses. The largest was formerly a post office and the end house, Tan-y-Bryn, was a general store.

The 1871 census returns show something of the population movements stimulated by the large scale development of the quarry. 516 people are listed for the Township of Maestrefnant between Rhiwerfa and Bryneglwys, and the village of Abergynolwyn. 136 of them worked at the quarry and if we add the few living nearby but not within the above area — mainly the hamlet of Cwrt — this accounts for barely half the Bryneglwys workforce. If another fifty lodged in the barracks there must have been up to a hundred more lodging in local houses during the week, an average approaching one per household. In Maestrefnant almost one quarter of the population was five years old or less, a striking reminder of how young couples were attracted into the area by the prospect of economic stability, created by the quarry company. Just over half of the 105 quarrymen resident in Abergynolwyn were born in Merioneth, thirty-one were from Montgomery and sixteen from Caernarvonshire. There were none from the Ffestiniog district.

At first sight the Company houses in the village resemble the terraces built in industrial towns all over Britain in the nineteenth century. But they are well

[4] PRO RG10 5689, 1871 Population Census for Merioneth.
[5] NLW Ms BRA 905 (1955) No. 40.

built, of slate slab with slate roofs of course, and will probably outlast many houses being built today. They are not overcrowded and the views all round are superb, so it is surprising that L. T. C. Rolt dismissed them so scathingly in *Railway Adventure:*

> On the south side of the village two short terraces eye each other across an unmade street which begins and ends nowhere. It looks as though a section had been arbitrarily chopped out of a mean street in any industrial city in the abortive hope that it might take root and grow.[6]

Hugh Roberts, a rockman who gave evidence at the 1894 inquiry into the Merioneth slate mines took a different view when he was asked:

> Have you good houses?
> Yes, they are excellent houses, or so they seem to me, compared with the huts in which men lived in my early days.
> How old are you?
> I am a widower and am not going to tell you my age. I am 63.[7]

Whatever the outward appearance of the village, a strong community spirit grew up and indeed flourishes today. It was largely a self-contained community and the people remained close to the land. The Company set aside plots in the village which the men rented for allotments at one farthing (.1p) per square yard per annum. They also rented land on which they kept a cow or two, and pigs. Hugh Roberts told the Inquiry that the letting of land and allotments was of the greatest advantage to the men. He was asked:

> Which two classes of workmen are the healthier, the men who work underground or those who work outside?
> The men who work outside, of course.
> Would you be surprised to hear that the reverse is true in the Festiniog district?
> I don't know about that, but they drink too much tea in Festiniog.
> Do you drink much tea here?
> No, we try to get milk here.

Allegations of excessive tea drinking were made much of at the Inquiry. Ellis Jones, a rockman from Aberllefenni, said that many quarrymen there kept a cow or two on land let by the Agent, and he stressed the value of milk in maintaining good health — 'I could not live on tea.' But in the cutting sheds the dust was blamed for indigestion and feelings of weakness, faint and thirst. Under these conditions, as well as underground where the atmosphere was frequently dense, dusty and unwholesome due to blasting operations it is no wonder that tea was drunk in generous measure.

As to their general diet, evidence was given at the Inquiry by a cookery demonstrator. She thought that the practice of paying wages monthly led some families to live in comparative luxury for the first week and live very scantily for the rest of the month. She believed that:

[6] L.T.C.Rolt, 'Railway Adventure', David and Charles 1961, p. 18.
[7] Report of the Departmental Committee upon Merionethshire Slate Mines, 1895.

> tea often served as breakfast, dinner and supper, accompanied only by bread and butter, and sometimes tinned meat . . . in some cases the women preferred to cook pancakes swimming in butter, with tea, instead of a good substantial dinner.

The County Medical Officer reported in April 1897 the following death rates: Llanegryn, 6.25 per 600 population; Llangelynin, 8.33 per 650; Llanfihangel (including Abergynolwyn) 26.15 per 960.[8] He was unable to account for the high rate in Abergynolwyn, which 'was not due to consumption or infectious disease'. Only five were attributed to heart disease, so the high rate was inexplicable 'unless the quarry was to blame. The sanitation at Abergynolwyn is far from perfect'. Meyrick Roberts contested these figures, claiming that there were four fewer deaths than reported. A month later another report by the M.O. stated that his recommendation concerning sanitary arrangements had been entirely ignored by the Talyllyn Railway Company. Night soil from the village houses was removed from the privies and loaded into wagons on the village tramway to be taken away for disposal by the T.R.

Mr. Caradog Jones remembered the part played by the tramway in his boyhood:

> Now the village was planned very well. There was a railway track running between the streets, and you could get your coal to the front of the house, from the truck to the coal bunker. I remember when my brother and I were at school, we used to jump into the truck and throw the coal into the open door. All the corporation depended on the railway for everything. It was a great day when the rope would snap and the trucks would come tumbling down. It was a great loss always.

Haydn Jones installed a small hydro-electric plant at Abergynolwyn in the 1920s to provide current for the houses. The electricity was supposed to be used for lighting only, the cost being included in the rent, no meters being installed. It was stipulated that only Osram tested bulbs were permitted, not more than one 40 watt bulb in each living room and one 20 watt in each bedroom. Ironing was allowed during specified two-hour periods each week! The supply was turned off if people used it for heating, or in summer when the water supply was short. Abergynolwyn was not connected to the National Grid until the 1970s.

Village life is recalled by Mr. Caradog Jones:

> There was a very close tie between the village and the quarry. The village was built in such a hurry and they wanted a lot of quarrymen, so they came from every direction, it was a mixture of people from different parts of Wales and some of the children of the old families are still here. They are quite talented people, I remember quite well some of them singing during dinner time in the barracks; they were competing in the National Eisteddfod of Wales. Others were reciting and I remember a few of them coming back winning first prize. They simply taught themselves, they didn't go to anybody, they were good musicians. During that period the chances of today weren't there and people couldn't afford their children to go to colleges and

[8] *Towyn-on-Sea and Merioneth County Times,* Bound volumes in Tywyn Public Library, 1896-8.

> so forth. It was a great loss to them but it was a gain to the village to have such people amongst them. I was only a young lad when I joined the mixed choir which went to Harlech festival with the London Symphony Orchestra coming over to play, I could sing Handel's *Messiah* when I was sixteen years of age. I give credit to them, I've got very great respect for the old generation that has gone, they were very good people. You could rely on them and I often ask myself what is our generation giving to the next one. I'm afraid we are falling short in that way but the old people gave a good example and I treasure it even today.

In modern times the village has expanded and a housing estate covers part of the allotments worked by the quarrymen. But it was essentially a typical village of the Slate Age whose inhabitants were born, lived, laboured, worshipped and were finally buried beneath the ubiquitous slate which gave them their livelihood.

APPENDIX 1

FATAL ACCIDENTS AT BRYNEGLWYS QUARRY

Name	*Date of accident*		*Cause of death*
Owen	7 Jul	1866	Fell 18 yards down a shaft.
William Owen	16 Apr	'77	Knocked over a ledge by falling rock whilst boring a hole. Fell 6 yards injuring spine. Died next day.
David Evans Hugh Jones	7 Dec	'77	After blasting, a piece of rock weighing 7 tons fell and crushed both men.
Edward Davies	16 Dec	'77	Fell 20 yards from landing stage whilst unhooking chains from wagon.
Unknown		1877	Killed by truck running away down an incline on the exit tramway.
John Watkin	2 Apr	'81	Trapped by a fall of earth whilst excavating for a new reservoir, probably above the Lower Mill.
Thomas Elias Rogers	19 Oct	'81	Got his coat caught in a rotating turbine shaft whilst examining the speed.
John Lewis	19 Sep	'87	Trapped by falling rock whilst excavating a cutting.
David Roberts	2 May	'88	Struck by a stone weighing 30 lbs falling from above his workplace.
Richard Davies	13 Aug	'89	Struck by a rockfall from a chamber roof.
David Evans	19 Feb	'90	Struck by unexpected fall of a block weighing about 25 tons from above his workplace.
Owen Ellis	28 Feb	'94	Fell about 17 yards when climbing down a chain being used to lower a block of slate.
Thomas O. Ellis	5 Nov	'94	Crushed by unexpected fall of hundreds of tons of rock from a chamber roof.

Name	*Date of accident*	*Cause of death*
David Owen	14 Jul '96	Fell down a shaft he had entered 'out of curiosity'.
David Davies	27 Jan '02	Fell backwards over a ledge when his crowbar slipped whilst barring a stone.
Edward Lewis	26 Sep '02	Crushed by unexpected fall of rock after the ledge he was standing on gave way.
Robert Owen	?1904	Fell over the end of a tip and rolled to the bottom.
Thomas Owen	? Jul '20	Fell about 7 yards, severely injuring his head.
Huw Roberts	?1928	Died after a rock fell and trapped his leg.

Details of deaths are reported by the Inspector of Mines for the years 1875-1914 only.

APPENDIX 2

QUARRY LEASEHOLDS

Date of lease	*Rights comprised in lease*	*Term*	*Rents and royalties*
12/11/1844	To remove slates, flags and stones from the lands known as Bryneglwys.	50 years from 12/11/1844	£40 fixed rent per annum plus compensation for damage to herbage.
31/12/1846	To quarry slates on Cantrybedd.	60 years from ?1846	Not known, probably $\frac{1}{12}$th royalty.
5/ 2/1866, 26/ 3/1866	Right to work slates and quarries in lands known as Cantrybedd, containing about 366 acres.	As to $\frac{6}{7}$ths 45 years from 25/3/1864. As to $\frac{1}{7}$th 40 years from 25/3/1867	$\frac{1}{15}$th of the slates obtained or at Lessor's option $\frac{1}{15}$th of market value of slates at quarry, or Rent of £200 p.a. in lieu at like option.
20/ 2/1866	Part of Cantrybedd Farm known as Cae Beudynewydd and piece of land for exit tramway. Mines and minerals therein.	45 years from 25/3/1864	£9 p.a. for Cae Beudynewydd and tramway land, $\frac{1}{12}$th of ores and minerals or $\frac{1}{12}$th of their value at Lessor's option.
1/ 5/1866	Slates, quarries and mines on Hendre Wallog; right to make a railway and use roads; right to use herbage and tip spoil.	45 years from 1/5/1866	£7 p.a. for herbage, $\frac{1}{15}$th of slates and minerals or at Lessor's option $\frac{1}{15}$th of value of slates and minerals, or at like option rent of £50 p. a.

Date of lease	*Rights comprised in lease*	*Term*	*Rents and royalties*
1/ 5/1866	Two-thirds of the slates, quarries, mines and minerals in mountain land on Ruck property.	21 years from 1/5/1866, renewable for 24 years on giving notice at minimum rent of £66 13s. 4d.	$\frac{2}{3}$rds of $\frac{1}{15}$th of slates and minerals or at Lessor's option $\frac{2}{3}$rds of $\frac{1}{15}$th of value or at like option £33 6s 8d.
2/ 9/1878	To work and remove slates, flags and stones in the lands known as Bryneglwys which contain about 439 acres.	32 years from 31/3/1878	£40 p.a. fixed rent and $\frac{1}{15}$th cash value of slates, subject to a minimum royalty of £100, until 30/9/1894. Royalty increased thereafter to £140 minimum.
3/ 9/1878	Ores and minerals under Bryneglwys.	32 years from 31/3/1878, determinable by notice from lessee.	$\frac{1}{12}$th sale price of minerals or at Lessor's option $\frac{1}{12}$th of minerals less expenses of carriage etc.
30/11/1908	Right to work slates and quarries in lands known as Cantrybedd, containing about 366 acres. (Renewal of 1866 leases).	From 25/3/1909 and 25/3/1907 until 31/3/1910	Same terms as 1866 leases.

Date of lease	*Rights comprised in lease*	*Term*	*Rents and royalties*
21/11/1911	To work slates in Bryneglwys.	30 years from 29/9/1911	
15/12/1911	To work quarries, slates, stones, ores and minerals in and upon Hendre Wallog. Two-thirds of the slates, rocks and stones in mountain land on Ruck property.	30 years from 1/12/1911	$\frac{1}{25}$th royalty on cash value of slates and a dead rent of £10 p.a. $\frac{2}{3}$rds of $\frac{1}{25}$th royalty on cash value of slates, dead rent of £5 p.a.
22/ 2/1912	Right to work slates and quarries at Cantrybedd.	30 years from 1/12/1911	$\frac{1}{25}$th royalty subject to a minimum of £50 p.a. in first year rising to £100 in 7th year. £12 10s annual rent for buildings, water and land for tipping.

APPENDIX 3

BRYNEGLWYS SLATES SHIPPED FROM ABERDYFI

Actual slate tonnages are recorded in the Cambrian Railways port account books for the years 1884-7; for 1895 onwards the tonnages are not quoted. By assuming that the ratio of cargo weight to registered tonnage is the same for both periods, a reasonable approximation should be obtained for these years. The results are shown below.

Year	*Bryneglwys output* *tons*	*Shipped from Aberdyfi* *tons*	*% of output shipped*
1884	7067	3913	55.4
1885	7006	3589	51.2
1886	5901	3797	64.3
1887	5374	3806	70.8
1895	5805	†2475	42.6
1896	4974	1687	33.9
1897	5819	1755	30.2
1898	5501	1558	28.3
1899	5385	1615	30
1900	5531	1122	20.3
1901	5383	1162	21.6
1902	6099	985	16.2
1903	5562	715	12.9
1904	6397	1117	17.5
1905	5723	2101	36.7
1906	3816	1852	48.5
1907	3531	769	21.8
1908	3366	—	—
1909	3046	193	6.3
1910	§	264	—
1911	—	—	—
1912	3100	284	9.2
1913	2721	—	—
1914	*2507	144	5.7
1915	*2116	85	4

† All figures after the year 1895 in this column are estimates.
§ Quarry closed.
* Estimated.

BIBLIOGRAPHY

Extended references to Bryneglwys Quarry are to be found in the following books:

BOYD, J. I. C. *Narrow Gauge Railways in Mid-Wales,* 2nd edn., Oakwood Press, 1970.

JONES, CARADOG, *Braslun o Hanes Pentref Abergynolwyn a Chwareli Bryneglwys,* O. Jones, Stryd y Bont, Llangefni.

ROLT, L. T. C. *Railway Adventure,* 2nd edn., David and Charles, 1961.

ROLT, L. T. C. (Ed.) *Talyllyn Century,* David and Charles, 1965.

For the maritime background, see

MORGAN, D. W. *Brief Glory,*

The development of the Union is dealt with in

JONES, MERFYN, *The North Wales Quarrymen's Union.*

General historical background of the industry is given in

LINDSAY, J., *A History of the North Wales Slate Industry,* David and Charles, 1974, which also contains a comprehensive bibliography.

Information on local quarries is given in

WILLIAMS, J. ARTHUR, *Trem yn Ôl,* Pwyllgor Cofnodion Cyngor Sir Meirion, Dolgellau, 1963.